THE EASY ASIAN COOKBOOK FOR SLOW COOKERS

The Easy ASIAN COOKBOOK for Slow Cookers

Family-Style Favorites from EAST, SOUTHEAST, and SOUTH ASIA

NANCY CHO

Photography by Hélène Dujardin

ROCKRIDGE
PRESS

For general information on our other products and services or to obtain technical support, please contact our Customer Care Department within the U.S. at (866) 744-2665, or outside the U.S. at (510) 253-0500.

Rockridge Press publishes its books in a variety of electronic and print formats. Some content that appears in print may not be available in electronic books, and vice versa.

TRADEMARKS: Rockridge Press and the Rockridge Press logo are trademarks or registered trademarks of Callisto Media Inc. and/or its affiliates, in the United States and other countries, and may not be used without written permission. All other trademarks are the property of their respective owners. Rockridge Press is not associated with any product or vendor mentioned in this book.

Photography © Hélène Dujardin, Food styling by Tami Hardeman

Illustration © Laura Gonzalez Barro/iStock

Cover photograph: Beef Pho Noodle Soup, p. 30; table of contents photograph, Red Chicken Curry, p.51; Chicken Arroz Caldo, p. 12; Spiced Cauliflower and Potatoes, p. 70; Burmese Chili Chicken, p. 97; Korean Pork Wraps, page 109; Indonesian Steamed Coconut Cupcake, p. 131; Stir-Fried Asparagus, p. 140

ISBN: Print 978-1-64152-002-7 | eBook 978-1-64152-003-4

To my husband, Brad, for being my number one fan and for washing all the slow cookers. To my sister, Denise, for being my best friend. To my son, Ben, for being my most honest critic.

CONTENTS

INTRODUCTION VIII

1 ASIAN SLOW COOKER 101 1

2 RICE & NOODLES 9

3 SOUPS & STEWS 21

4 CURRIES 47

5 VEGETABLES & TOFU 67

6 CHICKEN 81

7 MEAT 101

8 DESSERT 123

9 SIDE DISHES & SALADS 139

MEASUREMENT & CONVERSION TABLES 153

ASIAN PANTRY 154

REFERENCES 166

RECIPE INDEX 168

INDEX 170

INTRODUCTION

My parents worked long hours every weekday and weekend when my sister and I were growing up. Luckily, our grandmother lived with us and cooked every meal. Most times she was in the kitchen pickling vegetables, prepping ingredients, or stirring a pot over a hot stove for hours. Our counters always had large bowls of soaking beans, rice, or dried vegetables, like mushrooms, zucchini, radishes, and, if we were really lucky, fernbrake and bellflower root.

When I was a child, I had no interest in being in the kitchen. I was more interested in playing with my friends or doing almost anything else. It wasn't until I moved out of the house and had to eat my own cooking that I realized that I needed to learn how to cook. I came back begging my grandmother and mother to teach me, and it wasn't easy. They did not have any recipes nor did they measure anything. I had to learn by sight, smell, and, most of all, taste. On top of that, it was difficult to find ingredients, and no two ingredients tasted the same back then. Fermented sauces, like soybean and chili paste; kimchi; fish sauce; and *gochugaru* (Korean red chili flakes)—basically, the essential ingredients of Korean cooking—varied from one batch to another. Nowadays, more Asian ingredients are readily available at grocery stores or even online, and are becoming more consistent.

Now that I have my own family, it can be a challenge to get home-cooked meals on the table. With the combination of work and shuttling my son to school and all his activities, I regularly search for easy dinners. Having a home-cooked meal at the end of the day helps us regroup, catch our breath, and be together. But often, I simply do not have the time to be hovering over the stove or oven.

A friend of mine and I were sharing dinner ideas one day, and she mentioned that she loved using her slow cooker for stews, soups, and chilies. I did not grow up with a slow cooker in our home, and the first time I used one was to make nacho cheese sauce for an event at my son's elementary school. After that, the appliance was put away and forgotten. After our conversation, I remembered that my slow cooker was on the castaway shelf in the pantry and decided to take it out. Since my family eats a lot of Asian food, I started experimenting with Asian recipes that could be cooked in a slow cooker. This enabled me to make variations of our favorite entrées at home that took advantage of the ease and convenience of the slow cooker without compromising on Asian flavors.

In this book you will find well-known dishes from all the major regions of Asia. Along with favorite traditional home-style meals, you'll find some modern takes using authentic flavors. If cooking Asian cuisine is new to you, these easy-to-follow slow cooker recipes will take the pressure off. There's also a chapter dedicated to quick non-slow-cooker side dishes that can accompany many of the main dishes.

Many of the recipes in this book take less than 6 hours because overcooking meats and vegetables (even at a low temperature in the slow cooker) can result in a mushy texture, and this is not what we want to achieve. However, if you have a slow cooker that you can program to turn to warm after the cooking time has ended, you can set it up before leaving for work and have your meal ready when you get home.

I hope you will also dust off your slow cooker and find some new favorite meals here.

ASIAN SLOW COOKER 101

New to cooking Asian cuisine? The slow cooker can be a great first step to cooking and tasting a variety of Asian recipes. There are a few recipes in here that require some work on the stove top before transferring the ingredients to the slow cooker. If you have the time, you can get better results this way. A lot of the stove-top prep can be done the night before, and the techniques and steps are simple enough to take the guesswork out of cooking new recipes.

Benefits of Slow Cooking Asian Food

If you are familiar with cooking Asian cuisine, you'll find that using a slow cooker can make many dishes taste fantastic. There are so many soups and stews that are known to taste better the next day, but the slow cooker has the ability to lock in flavors and combine them at a low and steady temperature, creating delicious results the day of. Tough cuts of meat shine with a low-and-slow cooking method and come out fall-off-the-bone tender. The advantage to the slow cooker is that you can leave these tough meats alone and not worry about poking at them every so often.

I also found that a slow cooker is a great alternative to a steamer. Layering ingredients on the bottom, like lemongrass, garlic, and ginger, combined with the low and steady heat, infuses wonderful aromatics into the food. Not having to worry about adding water from time to time is also a bonus.

Although cooking can take longer in a slow cooker, it can actually be a time-saver for the home cook. There's a convenience factor that enables you to focus on other tasks while the slow cooker is cooking. Once a meal is in the slow cooker, you can run errands or focus on work rather than fuss over the stove or oven. In fact, you should refrain from opening the lid, as it can add to your cooking time. Also, a slow cooker comes in handy when you have to cook multiple dishes at the same time, as you can set something in the slow cooker while getting to work on other components. At our home, we love our side dishes!

The greatest advantage of the slow cooker is that it traps flavors, but it also retains liquids too. There is little evaporation, which is ideal for making broth-based soups, like Beef Pho Noodle Soup (page 30), Korean Oxtail Soup (page 22), and Shoyu Pork Ramen (page 41), where you want to accentuate the flavor and not have to keep adding water due to evaporation.

Since most liquids in a slow cooker do not evaporate, you can thicken up dishes just by using less liquid. And by using less, you won't dilute your dish with excess water and lose flavor. This is one of the reasons I have found that curries and stews work so well in slow cookers. There are a few sauces and curries that normally need a thickening agent when cooked on the stove. Never fear, you can still achieve this by turning the slow cooker to high for 15 minutes with a cornstarch or flour mixture to easily thicken your dish.

You will find that most recipes in this book involve easy prep that takes 15 or 20 minutes, like cutting up meats and vegetables. Recipes that require only quick knife work, such as dicing, slicing, julienning, and chopping, will be indicated by a "Quick Prep" label at the top of the page.

There are a few recipes in this book that benefit from a little more attention than just dumping and forgetting it. Some recipes call for pan searing first, because one thing most slow cookers cannot do is caramelize or brown ingredients. So if time allows, elevate your meal by sautéing and searing the ingredients before adding them to the slow cooker. This simple step will increase the richness and depth of your dish and give it a kick of flavor. You can always skip the stove top work if you are short on time, but in many cases the sautéing can be done the night before, and the slow cooker can do the rest the next day. Recipes that can be prepped the night before will be noted so you can plan ahead and then just throw the ingredients in the slow cooker in the morning.

Authentic Flavors from Your Slow Cooker

Not only is Asia the largest continent in the world, but it is also the biggest in terms of population. There is a vast range of ingredients and flavors from all the regions. You will find some common themes, but you'll also find unique differences from country to country. Although the slow cooker can make some ingredients deepen or mellow in flavor, it can also elevate flavors. Chiles can intensify in spiciness, which, if you can handle the heat, is wonderful in the food of many East and Southeast Asian countries. Ginger is a shining ingredient in the slow cooker. A little bit (especially grated) goes a long way, and you'll find that ginger is a staple ingredient in most Asian cuisine. Tomatoes thicken sauces beautifully with the low-and-slow method and work

FLAVOR MAP

This map shows the vast land of Asian countries, islands, and territories with quick references to the flavor profiles and ingredients of each country.

EAST ASIA

CHINA

Ingredients: soy sauce, garlic, ginger, vinegar, chiles, peppercorns, cloves

Flavors: spicy, salty, sweet, sour

JAPAN

Ingredients: shoyu, miso, kombu, mirin, *katsuobushi* (dried smoked bonito)

Flavors: salty, sweet, sour, bitter, umami

KOREA

Ingredients: soy sauce, *gochujang* (red chili paste), *doenjang* (fermented soybean paste), garlic, onion, sesame oil, *myeolchi* (dried anchovy)

Flavors: salty, spicy, sour, sweet

TAIWAN

Ingredients: vinegar, soy sauce, white pepper, rice wine, chiles

Flavors: salty, sour

SOUTHEAST ASIA

PHILIPPINES

Ingredients: garlic, tomato, soy sauce, onion, vinegar, pepper, fish sauce

Flavors: sweet, salty, sour

THAILAND

Ingredients: fish sauce, curry paste, lemongrass, Thai chiles, garlic, coriander, galangal

Flavors: sweet, salty, sour, creamy, bitter, spicy

VIETNAM

Ingredients: fish sauce, soy sauce, lemongrass, mint, cinnamon, star anise, lime

Flavors: sweet, salty, spicy, sour, bitter

INDONESIA

Ingredients: nutmeg, ginger, garlic, lemongrass, cinnamon, turmeric, coriander

Flavors: salty, sweet, spicy, sour, bitter

MALAYSIA

Ingredients: *kecap manis* (sweet soy sauce), *belacan* (dried fermented shrimp paste), galangal, tamarind, chiles

Flavors: salty, sweet, spicy, sour

SINGAPORE

Ingredients: soy sauce, lemongrass, chiles, garlic, tomato, belacan

Flavors: sweet, salty, spicy, sour

MYANMAR (BURMA)

Ingredients: fish sauce, *ngapi* (fish or shrimp paste), ginger, tomato, chiles

Flavors: salty, sour, spicy

CAMBODIA

Ingredients: black pepper, *prahok* (fermented fish paste), galangal, star anise, sweet basil, lemongrass

Flavors: salty, sweet, sour, bitter, citrus/acid

LAOS

Ingredients: *padek* (fish sauce), soy sauce, galangal, lemongrass, chiles

Flavors: salty, bitter, sour, spicy

SOUTH ASIA

INDIA

Ingredients: cardamom, cumin, coriander, ginger, cinnamon, cayenne pepper, turmeric

Flavors: spicy, sweet, sour

SRI LANKA

Ingredients: black pepper, coriander, chiles, cardamom, coconut, fennel, coriander

Flavors: spicy, sweet, sour, salty

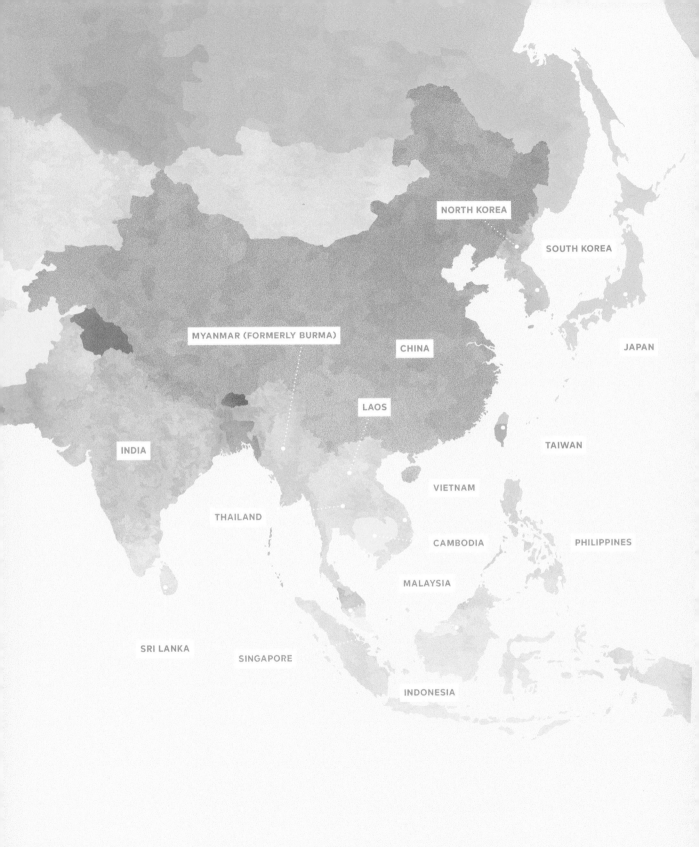

Know Your Slow Cooker

Slow cookers come in a variety of sizes and shapes. Sizes range from 2 to 6 quarts, and shapes include round, oval, and rectangular. Oval and rectangular slow cookers are good for big cuts of meat, ribs, and whole chickens. Although soups, stews, and curries can be cooked in any shape of slow cooker, I prefer to use a round one because there's less surface area to fill and it is easy to stir.

Modern slow cookers come with different controls. Some are very basic with a manual dial that turns to low, high, and warm. Some slow cookers also come with programmable timers that automatically switch to the warm setting when cooking is finished. This option gives you more flexibility in case you're running late or lose track of time. Lastly, there are slow cookers that have a multifunction cooking system. They can sauté, sear, roast, and slow cook so that you do not have to transfer ingredients from a pan to the slow cooker.

Most recipes in this book make 6 servings, so they were tested on 5- and 6-quart slow cookers with a removable insert. Whenever possible, the recipes in this book state low and high cooking times so that you can choose which time frame will work for you.

If you have a smaller slow cooker, such as a 2- to 4-quart model, you can halve the recipes. Just make sure you follow the general rule of thumb that the ingredients in your slow cooker should fill it between halfway and three-quarters full.

Using Your Slow Cooker: Dos and Don'ts

- **DO** prep your slow cooker by lightly coating it with cooking spray or oil to make cleaning easier.

- **DO** resist the urge to overseason. Slow cookers trap and intensify flavors from ingredients, so it's generally best to wait until the end of cooking to add salt.

- **DO** create your own steaming rack if you don't have one. Use aluminum foil coils or rolled-up foil balls and place them at the bottom of your slow cooker to replicate a steaming rack.

- **DO** make sure your slow cooker is between halfway and three-quarters full of ingredients. Any more or less can affect the quality and safety of your dish.

- **DO** read your manual and test the low and high temperatures of your slow cooker. Not all slow cookers are created equal.

- **DON'T** peek! Resist opening your slow cooker lid too often, especially in the early stages of cooking, when heat is building. Each time you open the lid will increase your cooking time by 15 to 20 minutes.

- **DON'T** put frozen food in your slow cooker. To ensure complete cooking and safe food temperatures during cooking, make sure all food is properly thawed before it goes in the slow cooker.

- **DON'T** use harsh cleaners or scrubbers when cleaning your slow cooker. Read the manual instructions on how to clean your slow cooker.

- **DON'T** reheat food in a slow cooker, as it can take too long to get to a safe temperature.

- **DON'T** add too much liquid. Little evaporation happens in the slow cooker.

CHICKEN ARROZ CALDO, PAGE 12

2

RICE & NOODLES

CHICKEN CONGEE   10

MUSHROOM JOOK   11

CHICKEN ARROZ CALDO   12

STICKY RICE IN LOTUS LEAF   13

BLACK BEAN SAUCE NOODLES   15

YELLOW MUNG BEANS & RICE   16

DRUNKEN NOODLES   17

CHICKEN LO MEIN   18

SHAN NOODLES   19

Rice is an important staple in Asian cuisine, and it accompanies most main dishes. Each country uses its own unique version and types of rice. For example, short-grain rice is commonly used in Korea and Japan, while medium- and long-grain rice are preferred in Chinese cuisine. In South Asia, basmati is commonly used, and you will find short-, medium-, and long-grain rice in Southeast Asia. However, sticky or glutinous rice is preferred in Laos and Cambodia.

The three rice porridges in this chapter represent three different flavor profiles, including ginger, sesame oil, and fish sauce. For the recipes that call for noodles, the noodles will need to be cooked separately, but this doesn't take very long and can be done just before serving. Meanwhile, let the sauces simmer in the slow cooker so the flavors come together. Sauces may need to thicken up, so a quick addition of starch at the end will help give them more body.

CHICKEN CONGEE

Prep time: 10 minutes

Cook time: 6 to 7 hours on low, 3 to 4 hours on high

Serves 6

CHINA

Congee is a savory Chinese comfort-food favorite for breakfast or lunch. I've had so many conversations about rice porridge and how people grew up eating it and what ingredients they used. The ginger shines in this congee, and the slow cooker helps make it stand out. This rice porridge is simple and fast to assemble. You can add a little or a lot of toppings depending on your mood.

1½ to 2 pounds boneless, skinless chicken thighs

1 cup long-grain rice

8 cups low-sodium chicken broth

2-inch piece fresh ginger, peeled and sliced

3 garlic cloves, smashed

2 teaspoons salt

2 scallions, both white and green parts thinly sliced

¼ cup chopped fresh cilantro

Hot sauce (like sriracha), for serving

Fried shallots, for serving

Roasted peanuts, chopped, for serving

Soy sauce, for serving

1. In the slow cooker, combine the chicken thighs, rice, broth, ginger, garlic, and salt.

2. Cover and cook on low for 6 to 7 hours, or on high for 3 to 4 hours.

3. When the rice is completely broken down, remove the ginger slices and discard.

4. Using two forks, break up the chicken into bite-size pieces and stir.

5. Add hot water or salt to your desired taste and consistency and stir to combine.

6. Ladle into bowls and top with scallions and cilantro. Serve hot with your choice of hot sauce, fried shallots, peanuts, and soy sauce.

TECHNIQUE TIP: I've set this on low for 8 hours before, so if you need to, you can cook congee a little longer.

Per Serving: Calories: 311; Total fat: 6g; Protein: 34g; Carbs: 27g; Fiber: 1g; Sugar: 0g; Sodium: 1,005mg

MUSHROOM JOOK

Prep time: 20 minutes

Cook time: 5 to 6 hours on low, 3 to 4 hours on high

Serves 6

KOREA

When I visited Seoul, one of the few restaurants that I went to more than a couple times for breakfast was a place that served only *jook*. Jook is the Korean version of rice porridge, and I seriously geeked out over all the different kinds of jook in Seoul. When I was a child, my mom would make this when it was frigid outside or when we had colds. The sesame oil and mushrooms are the flavor standouts for this rice porridge.

1 cup short-grain rice, rinsed and drained

2 teaspoons extra-virgin olive oil

2 teaspoons sesame oil

3 cups finely diced shiitake mushrooms

1 medium onion, finely diced

2 medium carrots, finely diced

1 zucchini, finely diced

8 cups vegetable broth

Soy sauce, for serving

2 scallions, both white and green parts thinly sliced

Sesame seeds, for garnish

Nori, cut into thin strips, for garnish

1. Add the rice to the slow cooker.

2. In a large pan, heat the olive oil and sesame oil over medium-high heat. Add the mushrooms and onion to the pan and sauté until soft, 3 to 5 minutes. Transfer to the slow cooker.

3. Add the carrots, zucchini, and broth to the slow cooker and stir.

4. Cover and cook on low for 5 to 6 hours, or on high for 3 to 4 hours.

5. If needed, add hot water to achieve the desired consistency, and stir to combine. Ladle into bowls and serve hot, topped with soy sauce, scallions, sesame seeds, and nori.

PREP IT RIGHT: You can chop the vegetables and sauté the mushrooms and onion the night before. Keep them in the fridge until you're ready to add them to the slow cooker.

Per Serving: Calories: 202; Total fat: 4g; Protein: 4g; Carbs: 38g; Fiber: 5g; Sugar: 6g; Sodium: 779mg

PHILIPPINES

CHICKEN ARROZ CALDO

Prep time: 15 minutes

Cook time: 6 to 7 hours on low, 3 to 4 hours on high

Serves 6

One day when I was comparing rice porridge notes with my friends, Arroz Caldo came up and I was intrigued. This Filipino version of rice porridge uses rice that is sautéed beforehand, and the shining ingredients are fish sauce, ginger, and lemon. If you don't have time to prepare all the garnishes, whatever you do, don't leave the lemon out. A squeeze of lemon brightens up this dish and brings a fresh and tangy contrast to the hearty rice and chicken.

1 to 1½ pounds boneless, skinless chicken thighs

1 tablespoon extra-virgin olive oil

1 small onion, diced

3 garlic cloves, minced

2-inch piece fresh ginger, peeled and thinly sliced

1 cup short-grain rice, rinsed and drained

4 cups chicken broth

1½ tablespoons fish sauce

3 cups water

Salt

2 scallions, both white and green parts thinly sliced, for garnish

Fried garlic, for garnish

Lemon wedges, for serving

Hard-boiled eggs, halved, for serving

1. In the slow cooker, arrange the chicken thighs.

2. In a medium pan, heat the olive oil over medium-high heat and add the onion, garlic, and ginger. Cook until the onion is softened, about 3 minutes.

3. Add the rice and cook until it becomes translucent, 3 to 4 more minutes.

4. Turn off the heat and transfer the rice mixture to the slow cooker. Add the broth, fish sauce, and water.

5. Cover and cook on low for 6 to 7 hours, or on high for 3 to 4 hours.

6. Using two forks, break the chicken into bite-size pieces and stir. Add hot water to your desired consistency, season with salt, and stir to combine.

7. Ladle into bowls and serve topped with scallions, fried garlic, lemon, and 1 or 2 hard-boiled egg halves.

INGREDIENT TIP: If you like more fish sauce, add ½ teaspoon at a time at the end of cooking to taste.

Per Serving: Calories: 304; Total fat: 8g; Protein: 28g; Carbs: 29g; Fiber: 1g; Sugar: 1g; Sodium: 984mg

STICKY RICE IN LOTUS LEAF

Prep time: 20 minutes, plus 2 hours to soak

Cook time: 8 to 10 hours on low, 5 to 6 hours on high

Serves 4

CHINA

This is one of my favorite dim sum dishes. It's a perfect little package of seasoned sticky rice and bites of sausage and mushroom. Traditionally, *lap cheong* (Chinese sausage) is used in this dish, but I use any cooked pork sausage when I'm in a pinch. Although dim sum is normally served during brunch time, I like making these parcels of deliciousness on weekend mornings before we head out for activities. When we come home, all I do is whip up a quick vegetable side dish to complement them. You can assemble the parcels at night and have them ready to eat in the morning, or you could put them in the slow cooker before work and have them waiting when you get home.

2 cups sticky rice or sweet rice

2 whole lotus leaves, soaked for 1 hour, rinsed, and cut in half, or 2 (12-inch) squares parchment paper, cut in half

Vegetable oil, for greasing, plus 1 tablespoon

1 teaspoon Shaoxing cooking wine

1 teaspoon sesame oil

1 teaspoon oyster sauce

2 teaspoons dark soy sauce

2 shallots, finely diced

1 tablespoon minced garlic

½ cup thinly sliced shiitake mushrooms

Cooking spray

1. In a large bowl, cover the sticky rice with water and soak for 2 hours or overnight.

2. Prepare the lotus leaves or parchment paper by lightly greasing each piece on one side with vegetable oil. Set aside.

3. Drain the rice and place in a medium bowl with the cooking wine, sesame oil, oyster sauce, and soy sauce, and stir to combine. Set aside.

4. In a medium pan, heat the remaining tablespoon of vegetable oil over medium-high heat.

5. Add the shallots, minced garlic, and mushrooms to the pan. Cook until tender and moisture has evaporated, 3 to 4 minutes. Add the mushroom mixture to the sticky rice and stir to combine.

> **CONTINUED**

Sticky Rice in Lotus Leaf

> **CONTINUED**

6 to 8 cabbage leaves
1 medium onion, quartered
6 garlic cloves
2-inch piece fresh ginger, peeled and sliced
2 cups water
½ cup sliced lap cheong (Chinese sausage) or pork sausage

6. Spray the slow cooker with cooking spray and place a rack on the bottom. If you do not have a rack, make a large coil about 2 inches thick using aluminum foil.

7. In the slow cooker on top of the rack or coil, in this order, layer the cabbage leaves, onion, garlic cloves, and ginger. Add the water.

8. To assemble the rice packages, spoon about ¼ cup of rice mixture onto the middle of a piece of lotus leaf or parchment paper. Add 3 or 4 slices of sausage on top of the rice, then top with another ¼ cup of rice to cover the sausage. Tightly fold the package and use kitchen twine to tie it together. Make 3 more packages.

9. Place the 4 packages in the slow cooker in one layer.

10. Cover and cook on low for 8 to 10 hours, or on high for 5 to 6 hours. Serve.

TIME-SAVING TIP: Omit the mushroom mixture and just wrap the seasoned sticky rice and sausage. It's still tasty! Also, you can skip the layer of aromatics (cabbage, onion, garlic cloves, and ginger) and place the parcels directly on the rack or foil coil. Adjust the amount of water so that it is not touching the parcels, and proceed with the recipe.

Per Serving: Calories: 205; Total fat: 9g; Protein: 5g; Carbs: 30g; Fiber: 2g; Sugar: 2g; Sodium: 318mg

BLACK BEAN SAUCE NOODLES

KOREA

Prep time: **20 minutes**

Cook time: **5 to 6 hours on low, or 2 to 3 hours on high**

Servings: **6**

Whenever we go out to eat *Jjajangmyeon*, I make sure to wear a dark shirt. It's either that or wear my napkin as a bib. The sauce is made out of black bean paste, *jjajang*, that is specific to this dish. You can buy jjajang at most Asian stores and can now find it easily online. In Seoul, people have this popular Korean-Chinese fusion dish delivered right to their door.

1 pound pork shoulder, cut into bite-size pieces

1 tablespoon cornstarch, plus ¼ cup if needed to thicken sauce

3 tablespoons vegetable oil

¾ cup plus 2 tablespoons jjajang (fermented black bean paste)

1½ tablespoons sugar

5 cups chicken stock

1 russet potato, cut into ½-inch cubes

1 large onion, cut into ½-inch pieces

2 zucchini, quartered and cut into ½-inch pieces

1 pound jjajangmyeon noodles or udon

1 English cucumber cut into matchsticks, for garnish

1. In a large bowl or resealable bag, place the pork and 1 tablespoon of cornstarch. Mix to combine, then transfer the pork to the slow cooker.

2. In a medium pan, heat the oil over medium-high heat. Add the jjajang and sugar to the pan, stirring constantly for 2 minutes. Turn off the heat and transfer the black bean sauce to the slow cooker.

3. Add the stock, potato, onion, and zucchini to the slow cooker. Mix to combine.

4. Cover and cook on low for 5 to 6 hours, or on high for 2 to 3 hours.

5. If you would like the sauce thicker, in a small bowl, combine the remaining ¼ cup of cornstarch with ½ cup water and mix well. With the slow cooker on high, add the cornstarch mixture and cook for another 15 minutes.

6. Prepare the noodles according to package directions. Drain, then divide among bowls.

7. Once the sauce thickens, serve over the noodles and garnish with the cucumber.

INGREDIENT TIP: The term *jjajang* derives from a Chinese word meaning "fried sauce." It's important to fry the sauce, but nowadays you can even find jjajang sauce that has already been fried.

Per Serving: Calories: 506; Total fat: 15g; Protein: 33g; Carbs: 61g; Fiber: 5g; Sugar: 12g; Sodium: 2,268mg

YELLOW MUNG BEANS & RICE

Prep time: **10 minutes**

Cook time: **5 to 6 hours on low, 3 to 4 hours on high**

Serves **6**

INDIA

A popular rice and dal dish in India this is a comforting meal that covers your carbs, protein, and fiber in one pot. I use *moong dal* (split yellow mung beans) here, but there are many variations using different types of dal. I usually add a dollop of plain yogurt on the side and even sneak in a small pat of butter on top of my serving when I feel like it.

2 tablespoons extra-virgin olive oil

1 cup basmati rice

1 cup moong dal (split yellow mung beans)

1 medium onion, sliced

1 tomato, diced

1 cinnamon stick

2 teaspoons ground cumin

1 teaspoon salt

1 teaspoon ground turmeric

4 cups water

1 teaspoon garam masala

Salt

1. Grease the sides and bottom of the slow cooker insert with the oil.

2. In a bowl, wash the rice and dal in cold water until the water runs clear. Drain and transfer to the slow cooker.

3. In the slow cooker, add the onion, tomato, cinnamon stick, cumin, salt, turmeric, and water.

4. Cover and cook on low for 5 to 6 hours, or on high for 3 to 4 hours.

5. When the rice and dal are cooked, sprinkle with the garam masala, season with salt, and serve.

LEFTOVERS TIP: If you have leftovers, the consistency may thicken after refrigerating. Add water to achieve your desired consistency before reheating in the microwave or on the stove. After reheating, add salt to taste.

Per Serving: Calories: 191; Total fat: 5g; Protein: 5g; Carbs: 32g; Fiber: 2g; Sugar: 2g; Sodium: 395mg

DRUNKEN NOODLES

Prep time: **15 minutes**

Cook time: **3 to 3½ hours on low, 1 to 2 hours on high**

Serves **5 or 6**

THAILAND

Pad Kee Mao is traditionally made in a wok, but here is a simplified version for the slow cooker. This is one of my favorite hangover remedy dishes, but oddly enough, it also goes well with a cold glass of light beer. Thai chiles are spicy, and I don't ever skimp on the spice!

Cooking spray

1 to 1½ pounds boneless, skinless chicken thighs, cut into ½-inch pieces

1 tablespoon cornstarch

5 garlic cloves, minced

3 tablespoons soy sauce

⅓ cup oyster sauce

2 teaspoons brown sugar

1 tablespoon fish sauce

½ teaspoon peeled and grated fresh ginger

2 or 3 Thai chiles, seeded and julienned (optional)

2 tablespoons water

8 pieces baby corn, halved lengthwise

3 scallions, both white and green parts cut into 3-inch lengths

2 shallots, thinly sliced

1 red bell pepper, seeded and thinly sliced

1½ cups loosely packed Thai basil leaves

1 pound flat wide fresh rice noodles

1. Lightly spray the slow cooker with cooking spray.

2. In a large bowl or resealable bag, combine the chicken and cornstarch. Mix well and transfer to the slow cooker.

3. In a small bowl, whisk together the garlic, soy sauce, oyster sauce, brown sugar, fish sauce, ginger, chiles (if using), and water. Pour the mixture into the slow cooker.

4. Cover and cook on low for 3 to 3½ hours, or on high for 1 to 2 hours.

5. Add the baby corn, scallions, shallots, bell pepper, and Thai basil. Stir well, cover, and cook on high for 5 to 10 minutes.

6. Cook the noodles according to package instructions. Drain and rinse the noodles, then add to the slow cooker. Stir to combine, and serve.

SUBSTITUTION TIP: Can't find rice noodles? Use wheat or egg noodles.

Per Serving: Calories: 334; Total fat: 9g; Protein: 31g; Carbs: 33g; Fiber: 2g; Sugar: 5g; Sodium: 1,345mg

CHICKEN LO MEIN

Prep time: **10 minutes**

Cook time: **4 to 6 hours on low, 2 to 3 hours on high**

Serves **6**

CHINA

Believe it or not, I never order chow mein or lo mein at a Chinese restaurant. I always get distracted by the large menu and order Peking duck or winter melon soup. Instead, we satisfy our lo mein craving at home with this simple recipe. Normally made in a wok, I adapted this dish for the slow cooker for times when I don't want to fuss over the stove.

Cooking spray

2 pounds boneless, skinless chicken thighs, cut into ½-inch strips

2 cups chicken stock

5 garlic cloves, minced

5 tablespoons soy sauce

2 tablespoons oyster sauce

2 teaspoons sesame oil

1 tablespoon brown sugar

¼ teaspoon white pepper

3 cups chopped baby bok choy

1 cup thinly sliced shallots

1 red bell pepper, seeded and thinly sliced

3 scallions, both white and green parts cut into 3-inch lengths

2 tablespoons cornstarch

3 tablespoons water

1 pound lo mein noodles

1. Lightly spray the slow cooker with cooking spray.

2. In the slow cooker, add the chicken thighs, stock, garlic, soy sauce, oyster sauce, sesame oil, brown sugar, and white pepper, and stir to combine.

3. Cover and cook on low for 4 to 6 hours, or on high for 2 to 3 hours.

4. Add the bok choy, shallots, bell pepper, and scallions, and stir to combine. Cook on high for 5 minutes.

5. In a small bowl, mix the cornstarch and water.

6. Add the cornstarch mixture to the slow cooker and stir. Cover and cook on high for another 10 minutes.

7. Cook the noodles according to package instructions. Drain and rinse the noodles, then add to the slow cooker. Stir to combine, and serve.

PREP IT RIGHT: You can do some early prep by chopping vegetables the night before.

SUBSTITUTION TIP: Can't find lo mein noodles? You can use spaghetti.

Per Serving: Calories: 905; Total fat: 52g; Protein: 40g; Carbs: 72g; Fiber: 4g; Sugar: 4g; Sodium: 1,543mg

MYANMAR

SHAN NOODLES

Prep time: 15 minutes

Cook time: 5 to 6 hours on low, 2 to 3 hours on high

Serves 5 or 6

There are different variations on this rice noodle dish, and it is oftentimes served with chicken broth and pickled mustard greens. Here is the dry version that highlights tomato, fish sauce, and ginger flavor profiles. I love adding an extra spoonful of peanuts on mine with a dash of lime juice and hot sauce.

2 tablespoons vegetable oil

2 medium onions, diced

¼ cup minced garlic

1-inch piece fresh ginger, peeled and minced

2 pounds boneless, skinless chicken thighs

6 tomatoes, diced

2 tablespoons fish sauce

1 teaspoon ground turmeric

1 teaspoon chili powder

4 tablespoons soy sauce, plus more if needed

1 tablespoon tomato paste

2 teaspoons sugar

¼ teaspoon salt, plus more if needed

½ cup water

1 pound large rice noodles

3 scallions, both white and green parts thinly sliced, for garnish

Chopped peanuts, for garnish

Pickled mustard greens, for serving (optional)

1. In a medium pan, heat the oil over medium-high heat. Add the onions, garlic, and ginger, and sauté until the onions are soft and turning a little golden, 3 to 5 minutes. Transfer to the slow cooker.

2. In the slow cooker, add the chicken, tomatoes, fish sauce, turmeric, chili powder, soy sauce, tomato paste, sugar, salt, and water, and gently stir together.

3. Cover and cook on low for 5 to 6 hours, or on high for 2 to 3 hours.

4. Cook the noodles according to package instructions. Drain, then divide between bowls.

5. Taste the sauce and add more soy sauce or salt, if needed. Spoon the sauce over the noodles and top with the scallions and chopped peanuts. Serve with a side of pickled mustard greens, if using.

INGREDIENT TIP: Shan noodles are usually served with pickled mustard greens, which can be found in most Asian markets.

Per Serving: Calories: 667; Total fat: 14g; Protein: 42g; Carbs: 93g; Fiber: 5g; Sugar: 9g; Sodium: 1,740mg

BEEF PHO NOODLE SOUP, PAGE 30

3

SOUPS & STEWS

KOREAN OXTAIL SOUP 22

BEEF SHORT RIB SOUP 24

TOM KHA GAI 26

KOREAN GINSENG CHICKEN SOUP 27

PUMPKIN SOUP 29

BEEF PHO NOODLE SOUP 30

SOYBEAN PASTE STEW 32

LENTIL SOUP 34

HOT-AND-SOUR SOUP 35

BEEF NILAGA 36

FILIPINO OXTAIL PEANUT STEW 37

KIMCHI STEW 39

SHOYU PORK RAMEN 41

LAKSA NOODLE SOUP 43

VIETNAMESE BEEF STEW 44

For so many Asians, soups and stews are not a winter seasonal thing but rather, are enjoyed year-round. On warm days, the slow cooker comes in handy when your soups and stews are simmering and you don't want to be hovering over the stove. The East Asian soups and stews represented here have deep, savory flavors, like Hot-and-Sour Soup, which highlights white pepper and sour tastes. The South Asian soups encompass layers of flavor with spices, and you can thank the aromatic herbs and spices for the full-flavored Southeast Asian soups and stews.

KOREA

KOREAN OXTAIL SOUP

Prep time: **20 minutes**

Cook time: **8 hours on high**

Serves **6**

Ggori Gomtang takes a long time to make over the stove to achieve a real bone broth flavor and super-tender meat, making it ideal for slow cooking. The soup is served with rice and kimchi on the side. Everyone seasons their own bowl with salt, pepper, and scallions at the table. My mom makes a spicy paste for those of us who wanted spiciness in their soup. I've included that here if you are looking for an extra kick. If you can't find oxtails, you can substitute short ribs, or make Beef Short Rib Soup (page 24) instead.

For the soup

3 to 4 pounds oxtails

5 ounces dangmyeon (sweet potato vermicelli or glass noodles) (optional)

4 scallions, both white and green parts thinly sliced, for serving

Salt, for serving

Freshly ground black pepper, for serving

For the spicy paste (optional)

4 garlic cloves, finely minced

3 scallions, both white and green parts thinly sliced

2 tablespoons gochugaru (Korean red chili flakes)

1 tablespoon fish sauce

1 teaspoon salt

1 teaspoon cracked black pepper

To make the soup

1. In a large pot, cover the oxtails with cold water. Bring to a boil over high heat for 10 minutes.

2. Reduce the heat and simmer for another 10 minutes. Drain the oxtails, rinse very well, and trim off any excess fat.

3. Transfer the oxtails to the slow cooker and add water until the slow cooker is two-thirds full.

4. Cover and cook on high for 8 hours. When cooking is complete, skim any solids or oil from the surface.

5. Cook the noodles, if using, according to package directions. Drain, then place a small handful of noodles in each bowl.

6. Ladle the oxtail soup over the noodles. Serve alongside scallions, salt, pepper, and a side of rice.

To make the spicy paste, if using

In a small bowl, combine the garlic, scallions, gochugaru, fish sauce, salt, and pepper. Mix until it develops a paste-like consistency. Serve on the side and add a small spoonful (or more) to your soup if desired.

OPTION TIP: If you want a milkier broth, cook the oxtail bones longer in order to extract more of the bone marrow. Just take off the cooked oxtail meat, return the bones to the slow cooker, and keep cooking.

Per Serving: Calories: 750; Total fat: 40g; Protein: 94g; Carbs: 1g; Fiber: 0g; Sugar: 0g; Sodium: 588mg

BEEF SHORT RIB SOUP

Prep time: 20 minutes, plus 1 to 2 hours to soak
Cook time: 8 to 9 hours on low, 4 to 5 hours on high
Serves 5 or 6

KOREA

Although there is a soaking-and-parboiling process for the ribs, *Galbi-Tang* is easy to make, and everyone seasons their own soup at the table. Soaking and parboiling help get rid of the blood and any impurities from the ribs. When I'm in the mood, I make a spicy paste to add to the soup. This isn't traditional, but I included the paste recipe here as an option for a spicier soup. Galbi-Tang pairs very well with a side of kimchi.

For the soup

4 pounds beef short ribs, rinsed and fat trimmed
1 medium onion, quartered
3 large scallions, halved crosswise
6 garlic cloves
1 pound Korean radish or daikon, peeled and cut into 1-inch cubes
6 cups water, plus 2 cups hot water
5 ounces dangmyeon (sweet potato vermicelli or glass noodles) (optional)
4 scallions, both white and green parts thinly sliced, for serving
Salt, for serving
Freshly ground or cracked black pepper, for serving
Soy sauce, for serving

To make the soup

1. In large bowl, cover the ribs with water and soak for 1 to 2 hours to draw out the blood, changing the water once during soaking. Drain and rinse the ribs.

2. In a large stockpot, cover the ribs with water. Bring to a boil over medium-high heat and cook for 20 minutes. Drain and rinse the ribs under cold water to cool.

3. In the slow cooker, combine the ribs, onion, halved scallions, garlic, radish, and 6 cups water.

4. Cover and cook on low for 8 to 9 hours, or on high for 4 to 5 hours.

5. Remove the ribs and radish from the slow cooker and set aside. Discard the onion, scallions, and garlic. Using a spoon and a fine-mesh strainer, skim the fat and solids from the soup.

6. Return the ribs and radish to the slow cooker and add 2 cups hot water. Cover and set on high for 15 minutes.

7. Meanwhile, cook the noodles, if using, according to package directions. Drain, then place a small handful in each bowl.

8. Ladle the short rib soup over the noodles. Serve alongside the sliced scallions, salt, pepper, soy sauce, and a side of rice.

For the spicy paste (optional)

2 tablespoons gochugaru
    (Korean red chili flakes)
2 tablespoons soy sauce
2 teaspoons sesame oil
1 teaspoon salt
1 teaspoon freshly ground
    black pepper

To make the spicy paste, if using

In a small bowl, mix the gochugaru, soy sauce, sesame oil, salt, and pepper. Serve alongside the soup.

PREP IT RIGHT: The ribs can be soaked the night before. After soaking and rinsing, store in an airtight container overnight until ready to add to the slow cooker.

OPTION TIP: To achieve a clearer soup, pour the broth through a fine-mesh strainer lined with cheesecloth into a large bowl or stockpot in step 5, then return it to the slow cooker.

TECHNIQUE TIP: Some people opt for a 2-day process when preparing this soup by refrigerating the broth overnight in order to easily scoop out the fat that solidifies on top. Store the broth separately from the ribs and radish overnight in the refrigerator. When the fat solidifies, scoop it out and reheat the broth in a pot over the stove along with the ribs and radish.

Per Serving: Calories: 1,446; Total fat: 132g; Protein: 54g; Carbs: 8g; Fiber: 2g; Sugar: 3g; Sodium: 218mg

THAILAND

TOM KHA GAI

Prep time: **10 minutes**

Cook time: **5 to 6 hours on low, 3 to 4 hours on high**

Serves **4 or 5**

Although this is a soup, Tom Kha Gai is traditionally eaten with a side of rice. It's not thick like a curry, but the coconut milk makes this broth rich and creamy. Cooking coconut milk in a slow cooker for a long time can curdle it, so add it at the end, on high for 15 minutes. The hardest thing about this recipe is finding galangal and kaffir leaves. You can use the substitutions suggested below, and it'll still taste great, but if you can, get the real thing.

1 to 1½ pounds boneless, skinless chicken thighs, cut into ½-inch pieces

3 cups chicken broth

3 stalks lemongrass, tough outer layers removed, lightly pounded and cut into 3-inch diagonal sections

2-inch piece fresh galangal, peeled and thinly sliced

6 to 8 kaffir lime leaves, lightly bruised

¼ cup fish sauce, plus more if needed

3 or 4 Thai bird's eye chiles, lightly pounded

2 buna-shimeji mushroom clusters, bases removed, or 8 ounces shiitake mushrooms, thinly sliced

2 Roma tomatoes, cut into ½-inch pieces

1 (13.5-ounce) can coconut milk

4 tablespoons lime juice, divided

2 shallots, thinly sliced

4 tablespoons chopped fresh cilantro, divided

Salt (optional)

1. In the slow cooker, combine the chicken, broth, lemongrass, galangal, kaffir leaves, fish sauce, chiles, mushrooms, and tomatoes.

2. Cover and cook on low for 5 to 6 hours, or on high for 3 to 4 hours.

3. Add the coconut milk, 2 tablespoons of lime juice, shallots, and 3 tablespoons of cilantro. Cook on high for 15 minutes.

4. Turn off the heat and season with fish sauce, salt, or the remaining 2 tablespoons of lime juice to taste.

5. Divide into bowls and garnish with the remaining 1 tablespoon of cilantro. Serve with a side of jasmine rice.

SUBSTITUTION TIP: Galangal can be substituted with fresh ginger. Kaffir leaves can be substituted with lime peels. Use 6 to 8 hearty lime peel slices using a peeler.

Per Serving: Calories: 489; Total fat: 31g; Protein: 42g; Carbs: 15g; Fiber: 5g; Sugar: 8g; Sodium: 2,136mg

KOREAN GINSENG CHICKEN SOUP

KOREA

Prep time: 20 minutes, plus 1 hour to soak

Cook time: 8 hours on low, 4 hours on high

Serves 3 to 6

We used to fight over the rice that is cooked inside the chicken, so now we use a few Cornish hens to avoid any arguments. *Samgyetang* is usually eaten during the hot summer, and Koreans eat it to beat the heat and to boost energy and the immune system. Salt is served on the table so you can season your own broth, and the dipping sauce is for the chicken.

For the soup

¾ cup glutinous sweet rice

3 Cornish hens, giblets removed

9 garlic cloves

10 dried jujubes

2 large fresh or dried ginseng roots

10 chestnuts, peeled (optional)

3 scallions, white parts for soup and green parts thinly sliced, for garnish

To make the soup

1. In a small bowl, soak the rice for at least 1 hour or as long as overnight. Drain and set aside.

2. Rinse the inside and outside of each hen, then dry with paper towels.

3. Place 3 garlic cloves inside the cavity of each hen, then stuff each three quarters of the way full with rice, allowing room for the rice to expand.

4. Close each cavity using skewers or toothpicks and tie with kitchen twine to hold shut.

5. Arrange the hens in the slow cooker breast-side up.

6. Add the jujubes, ginseng, chestnuts (if using), white parts of the scallions, and enough water to just cover the hens.

7. Cover and cook on low for 8 hours, or on high for 4 hours.

8. Skim any solids from the surface. Discard the scallions.

9. To serve, place each hen into a bowl, or remove the meat from the hens and divide among bowls, and ladle broth on top. Garnish with the green parts of the scallions, and serve with the dipping sauce.

> **CONTINUED**

Korean Ginseng Chicken Soup

> **CONTINUED**

For the dipping sauce

2 teaspoons salt

1 teaspoon pepper

1 tablespoon sesame oil

To make the dipping sauce

In a small bowl, combine the salt, pepper, and sesame oil. Divide the sauce among individual small bowls, one for each serving.

OPTION TIP: You can use 1 small whole chicken instead of 3 Cornish hens. Stuff all the rice into the chicken cavity and fill the slow cooker halfway with water. Make sure the chicken is cooked to 165°F.

SUBSTITUTION TIP: If you can't find jujubes, you can substitute dried dates in this recipe. However, because they are sweeter than jujubes, cut the number to 6 dates.

Per Serving: Calories: 577; Total fat: 29g; Protein: 33g; Carbs: 45g; Fiber: 2g; Sugar: 0g; Sodium: 1,661mg

PUMPKIN SOUP

Prep time: 15 minutes

Cook time: 5 to 6 hours on low, 2 to 3 hours on high

Serves 6

SRI LANKA

Wattakka Soup is a delicious pumpkin soup that is creamy and has a hint of curry and sweetness. This simplified version is very easy to make, and you can do most of the prep the night before. Cutting up the pumpkin is what will take the most time, so get those forearm muscles working!

6 to 7 cups sugar pumpkin, peeled, seeded, and cubed

4 garlic cloves

1 teaspoon peeled, minced fresh ginger

1 medium onion, sliced

2 teaspoons curry powder

¼ teaspoon ground cinnamon

5 cups low-sodium chicken or vegetable broth

1 tablespoon brown sugar

½ cup heavy cream

Salt

Freshly ground black pepper

1. In the slow cooker, combine the pumpkin, garlic, ginger, onion, curry powder, cinnamon, and broth.

2. Cover and cook on low for 5 to 6 hours, or on high for 2 to 3 hours.

3. Use an immersion blender to process the soup until smooth.

4. Add the brown sugar and heavy cream. Stir to combine. Adjust heat to high and cook for an additional 10 to 15 minutes, until the cream is heated through and the flavors meld.

5. Season with salt and pepper and serve.

TECHNIQUE TIP: If you do not have an immersion blender, use a regular blender to blend the soup and pour it back into the slow cooker to finish the cooking process.

OPTION TIP: Garnish this soup with croutons or julienned fresh mint leaves.

SUBSTITUTION TIP: If you can't find sugar pumpkin, try this recipe with butternut squash or kabocha instead.

Per Serving: Calories: 135; Total fat: 8g; Protein: 4g; Carbs: 15g; Fiber: 1g; Sugar: 4g; Sodium: 97mg

BEEF PHO NOODLE SOUP

Prep time: **20 minutes**

Cook time: **8 to 9 hours on low, 4 to 5 hours on high**

Serves **5 or 6**

VIETNAM

Traditionally, *Pho Bo* is made with beef marrow and knucklebones, which must be boiled first to allow for the impurities to be released. I've skipped that step here by going straight for brisket. If you're in a rush, you can throw everything in the slow cooker, but taking the extra few minutes to toast the spices and roast the onions and ginger will release more of the aromatics into your broth. Using this simplified slow-cooker method enables our family to eat pho all the time.

1 medium onion, quartered

2-inch piece fresh ginger, peeled and halved lengthwise

3 green cardamom pods

1 cinnamon stick

3 whole star anise

1 to 1½ pounds beef brisket

3 garlic cloves, smashed

2 tablespoons fish sauce, plus more if needed

2 teaspoons sugar

6 cups low-sodium beef broth

3 cups water

Salt

14 ounces rice noodles

8 ounces top round steak, uncooked and very thinly sliced crosswise

Fresh Thai basil, for serving

Fresh cilantro, for serving

Fresh mint leaves, for serving

Mung bean sprouts, for serving

Jalapeños, seeded and thinly sliced, for serving

Lime wedges, for serving

Hoisin sauce, for serving

Sriracha, for serving

1. Preheat the oven to 425°F.

2. On a baking sheet, arrange the onion and ginger and roast until lightly charred, about 10 minutes. Alternatively, you can pan roast them on the stove in a lightly oiled pan over medium-high heat.

3. In a small, dry skillet over medium heat, toast the cardamom pods, cinnamon stick, and star anise for 3 to 4 minutes.

4. In the slow cooker, combine the roasted onion and ginger with the toasted spice mixture. Add the beef brisket, garlic, fish sauce, sugar, beef broth, and water.

5. Cover and cook on low for 8 to 9 hours, or on high for 4 to 5 hours.

6. Skim any solids or fat from the surface of the soup. Strain the soup through a fine-mesh sieve into a large stockpot. Place the pot on the stove over medium-low heat to keep the broth warm.

7. Remove the brisket from the sieve and slice it thinly across the grain. Discard everything else from the sieve.

8. Season the broth with additional fish sauce or salt, if desired.

9. Cook the rice noodles according to package instructions. Drain, then divide the noodles among bowls.

10. In each bowl, place several slices of brisket and a few slices of the raw top round on top of the noodles. Pour broth into each bowl.

11. Serve alongside Thai basil, cilantro, mint, bean sprouts, jalapeños, lime wedges, hoisin sauce, and sriracha.

PREP IT RIGHT: To save time, prep the aromatics and spices (steps 1 to 3) the night before, and refrigerate until ready to use.

Per Serving: Calories: 364; Total fat: 9g; Protein: 44g; Carbs: 24g; Fiber: 1g; Sugar: 2g; Sodium: 1,143mg

KOREA

SOYBEAN PASTE STEW

Prep time: **25 minutes**

Cook time: **6 to 7 hours on low, 3 to 4 hours on high**

Serves **6**

Doengang Jigaeew is a staple in most Korean households. Doenjang is Korean fermented soybean paste and is full of umami flavor. It's also a little pungent—I'd call it the much bolder and saltier version of miso. Doenjang is strong not only in flavor but in aroma, like some cheeses. Growing up, we used to call this stew "stinky pot" and then dove into a hot bowl of its yummy goodness. Making soups and stews out of doenjang mellows the flavor a little, but it still retains its punch.

6 cups boiling water

12 large myeolchi (dried anchovies), cleaned inside

4-inch-square dried konbu (kelp)

1 cup gluten-free doenjang (Korean fermented soybean paste)

1 to 2 teaspoons gochugaru (Korean red chili flakes)

1 cup diced onion

4 garlic cloves, minced

3 cups hobak (Korean gray squash), cut into ½-inch slices

2 cups thinly sliced shiitake mushrooms

1 (14-ounce) package tofu, drained and cut into 1-inch cubes

1 jalapeño, cut into ¼-inch slices (optional)

1 cup shrimp, peeled, deveined, and cut into ½-inch pieces (optional)

2 scallions, both white and green parts sliced

1. In the slow cooker, combine the water, myeolchi, and konbu.

2. Cook on high for 15 minutes. Discard the myeolchi and konbu.

3. Add the doenjang and gochugaru, and mix to combine. Add the onion, garlic, hobak, mushrooms, tofu, and jalapeño, if using.

4. Cover and cook on low for 6 to 7 hours, or on high for 3 to 4 hours.

5. Add the shrimp, if using, and cook on high for 15 minutes.

6. When the shrimp are pink and firm, add the scallions and cook for 1 minute longer, until just wilted. Serve with a side of rice.

INGREDIENT TIP: Check the label to make sure your doenjang does not contain any gluten. Gluten-free doenjang is available online.

SUBSTITUTION TIP: If you can't find myeolchi, use 2 tablespoons fish sauce in its place. If you are unable to find hobak squash, substitute zucchini.

TIME-SAVING TIP: Make the broth (steps 1 and 2) up to 5 days in advance and store refrigerated in an airtight container until ready to use.

DIET TIP: You can easily make this dish vegetarian by using vegetable stock instead of water, leaving out the dried anchovies, and omitting the shrimp.

Per Serving: Calories: 416; Total fat: 13g; Protein: 46g; Carbs: 22g; Fiber: 6g; Sugar: 5g; Sodium: 4,321mg

INDIA

LENTIL SOUP

Prep time: 10 minutes

Cook time: 4 to 5 hours on low, 2 to 3 hours on high

Serves 5 or 6

You can use other kinds of lentils, but I prefer yellow lentils for *Dal Shorva*. I find that yellow lentils have a more delicate flavor and are a little softer when cooked. Whatever you do, don't forgo the lemon juice and garam masala at the end. They really enhance and brighten the dish.

Cooking spray

1 tablespoon extra-virgin olive oil or vegetable oil

1 medium onion, finely diced

3 garlic cloves, minced

1½ teaspoons peeled and grated fresh ginger

2 cups yellow lentils

1 teaspoon ground cumin

¼ teaspoon ground cardamom

1 teaspoon ground coriander

½ teaspoon ground turmeric

1½ teaspoons salt

5 cups water

½ teaspoon garam masala

Juice of 1 lemon

½ cup chopped fresh cilantro, for garnish

1. Spray the slow cooker lightly with cooking spray.

2. In a medium pan, heat the oil over medium-high heat. Add the onion, garlic, and ginger, and cook until onion is soft, 3 to 5 minutes.

3. In the slow cooker, combine the onion mixture, lentils, cumin, cardamom, coriander, turmeric, salt, and water. Stir to combine.

4. Cover and cook on low for 4 to 5 hours, or on high for 2 to 3 hours.

5. Stir in the garam masala and lemon juice, and garnish with the cilantro. Serve with bread or basmati rice on the side.

SUBSTITUTION TIP: You can use red lentils if you cannot find yellow lentils, but you may have to increase the cooking time by 1 to 2 hours on low or by 1 hour on high.

TIME-SAVING TIP: If you're short on time, you can skip the sautéing of the onions, garlic, and ginger in step 2 and just add them to the slow cooker with the rest of the ingredients in step 3.

Per Serving: Calories: 310; Total fat: 4g; Protein: 20g; Carbs: 49g; Fiber: 24g; Sugar: 3g; Sodium: 1,865mg

HOT-AND-SOUR SOUP

Prep time: 15 minutes

Cook time: 5 to 7 hours on low, 2 to 3 hours on high

Serves 6 or 7

CHINA

Want to know what the Hot-and-Sour Soup trifecta is? It's vinegar, white pepper, and soy sauce. Get that balance right and you've got the best recipe for this popular soup. For more vinegar and pepper flavor, I add them at the end of cooking. I also add a little cornstarch at the end gives this soup the right amount of body without making it too dense. Cooking this soup in the slow cooker means that you can have it on warm all day and grab a bowl of it whenever you want.

8 cups low-sodium chicken broth or vegetable broth

2½ tablespoons light soy sauce

3 tablespoons white vinegar, divided

¾ cup thinly sliced shiitake mushrooms

¾ cup thinly sliced wood ear mushrooms

7 ounces soft or regular tofu, cut into ¼-inch strips

¾ cup bamboo shoots, cut into thin strips

¼ cup cornstarch

¼ cup water

½ teaspoon white pepper

Salt (optional)

Soy sauce (optional)

1 scallion, both white and green parts thinly sliced, for garnish

1. In the slow cooker, combine the broth, soy sauce, 2 tablespoons of vinegar, shiitake mushrooms, wood ear mushrooms, tofu, and bamboo shoots.

2. Cover and cook on low for 5 to 7 hours, or on high for 2 to 3 hours.

3. In a small bowl, mix the cornstarch and water. Slowly add the cornstarch mixture to the slow cooker. Cover and cook on high for 15 minutes.

4. Add the white pepper and remaining 1 tablespoon of vinegar, and stir to combine.

5. If needed, season with salt or soy sauce. Serve garnished with the scallion.

INGREDIENT TIP: I use soft tofu (not silken) and carefully slice it. Soft tofu has a silky texture but holds some of its shape. It lends itself well to the slow cooker and soaks up all the flavors.

TECHNIQUE TIP: This soup has a flexible cooking time, so if you need to, you can keep it in the slow cooker for at least an extra hour.

Per Serving: Calories: 107; Total fat: 2g; Protein: 7g; Carbs: 11g; Fiber: 2g; Sugar: 1g; Sodium: 561mg

PHILIPPINES

BEEF NILAGA

Prep time: **25 minutes**

Cook time: **6 to 7 hours on low, 3 to 4 hours on high**

Serves **6**

Beef Nilaga in Tagalog translates to "boiled or stewed beef." Using a slow cooker is a great method for bringing out the beef flavor in the broth and achieving tender beef. I know it sounds odd, but the bananas are soft and a little sweet, and go well in the savory broth. Make sure you use a cooking type of banana, like saba or plantains.

2 tablespoons vegetable oil, divided

2 pounds beef chuck roast, cut into 1½- to 2-inch cubes

1 medium yellow onion, finely diced

3 or 4 medium Yukon gold potatoes, peeled and cut into 1-inch cubes

4 medium carrots, peeled and cut into 1- to 1½-inch pieces

1 tablespoon whole black peppercorns

2 tablespoons fish sauce, plus 2 teaspoons

1 teaspoon salt

5 cups water

2 cups sliced pechay or bok choy leaves

1 to 2 saba bananas or plantains, cut into thick slices (optional)

Salt

Juice of 1 lemon

1. In a large pan, heat 1 tablespoon of oil over medium-high heat. Add the beef to the pan and brown on all sides, about 5 minutes.

2. Transfer the beef to the slow cooker and return the pan to the stove. Lower the heat to medium.

3. Add the remaining 1 tablespoon of oil to the pan. Add the onion and sauté until slightly brown and soft, 3 to 5 minutes. Turn off the heat and transfer the onion to the slow cooker.

4. In the slow cooker, add the potatoes, carrots, peppercorns, 2 tablespoons of fish sauce, salt, and water.

5. Cover and cook on low for 6 to 7 hours, or on high for 3 to 4 hours.

6. Gently stir in the pechay and bananas, and cook on high for 10 to 15 minutes. Stir in the salt.

7. In a small bowl, mix the lemon juice and remaining 2 teaspoons of fish sauce together for dipping.

8. Ladle the soup into bowls and serve with a bowl of rice and dipping sauce on side.

PREP IT RIGHT: You can chop the vegetables and beef the night before and save 15 minutes.

Per Serving: Calories: 528; Total fat: 32g; Protein: 30g; Carbs: 29g; Fiber: 5g; Sugar: 5g; Sodium: 1,198mg

FILIPINO OXTAIL PEANUT STEW

Prep time: **30 minutes**

Cook time: **8 to 10 hours on low, 4 to 5 hours on high**

Serves **6**

PHILIPPINES

Super-tender oxtail meat with a thick and savory peanut sauce? I'm in. *Kare Kare* has a distinct but not overpowering peanut flavor and tends to be cooked without salt so that you can eat it with *bagoong alamang*, a salty shrimp paste, on the side. This is definitely one of those dishes you would think takes hours over the stove, but really, you let the slow cooker do its thing. We devour this stew in our home with a side of rice.

3 to 3½ pounds oxtails

1 tablespoon vegetable oil

1 large onion, diced

6 garlic cloves, minced

3 to 5 cups beef broth

1½ teaspoons achiote or annato powder

2 cups Chinese long beans, cut into 1-inch lengths, or regular green beans

2 cups pechay or bok choy, cut into large pieces

¾ cup creamy peanut butter

¼ cup all-purpose flour

¼ cup water

Bagoong alamang (salted shrimp paste), for serving (optional)

1. In a large pot, cover the oxtails with cold water. Bring to a boil over high heat for 10 minutes. Reduce the heat and simmer for another 10 minutes.

2. While the oxtails are boiling, in a medium pan, heat the oil over medium-high heat.

3. Add the onion and garlic to the pan and cook until softened, 3 to 5 minutes.

4. Transfer the onion mixture to a bowl, cover, and set aside in the refrigerator.

5. Drain the oxtails, rinse very well, and trim any excess fat.

6. In the slow cooker, arrange the oxtails and add just enough broth to reach the top of the oxtails. Add the achiote powder.

7. Cover and cook on low for 8 to 10 hours, or on high for 4 to 5 hours.

> **CONTINUED**

Filipino Oxtail Peanut Stew

> **CONTINUED**

8. Using a large spoon, remove excess fat from the broth, then add the onion mixture, long beans, pechay, and peanut butter to the slow cooker, and stir to combine.

9. In a small bowl, mix the flour and water together into a smooth slurry. Stir the slurry into the slow cooker, cover, and cook on high for 15 minutes.

10. Serve in bowls, with rice and bagoong alamang, if using, on the side.

INGREDIENT TIP: You can add salt or fish sauce at the end if you prefer not to use bagoong alamang.

SUBSTITUTION TIP: If you can't find oxtails, substitute beef shank or short ribs instead. Annato powder is available at many well-stocked supermarkets, but if you can't find it, substitute 1 teaspoon paprika mixed with ½ teaspoon turmeric.

PREP IT RIGHT: You can boil the oxtails, chop the vegetables, and sauté the onion and garlic the night before, and store them separately in the refrigerator until you are ready to throw them into the slow cooker.

Per Serving: Calories: 923; Total fat: 53g; Protein: 96g; Carbs: 18g; Fiber: 4g; Sugar: 6g; Sodium: 1,316mg

KIMCHI STEW

Prep time: 20 minutes

Cook time: 5 to 6 hours on low, 2 to 3 hours on high

Serves 6

KOREA

One of the things I love about kimchi is that there's a dish for every stage of its life. When the kimchi starts to get a little old and translucent, it's time to make *Kimchi Jjigae*. You can use any stage of kimchi, but it's best when your kimchi has aged. We grew up with a separate kimchi fridge, so you know we had this stew a lot. Most Kimchi Jjigae recipes use an anchovy stock as the base, but to cut out those extra steps, I make mine with a little fish sauce and chicken broth instead. When cooked in the slow cooker, the flavors of all the ingredients blend nicely together. Serve with a side of rice and you've got yourself a satisfying, fiery meal.

1 tablespoon vegetable oil

1 to 1½ pounds pork shoulder, cut into bite-size pieces

4 cups kimchi

3 garlic cloves, minced

½ cup kimchi juice or water

¼ cup gochujang (Korean red chili paste)

2 teaspoons sugar

½ teaspoon salt

1 teaspoon fish sauce

4 cups low-sodium chicken broth

1 (14-ounce) package regular or firm tofu, cut into ½-inch cubes

Salt

1 teaspoon sesame oil

3 scallions, both white and green parts thinly sliced, for garnish

1. In a large pan, heat the oil over medium-high heat. Add the pork and sear for about 3 minutes. Transfer the pork to the slow cooker, reserving the leftover oil in the pan.

2. Add the kimchi and garlic to the pan and cook for about 3 minutes, or until it is slightly softened. Transfer to the slow cooker.

3. Add the kimchi juice, gochujang, sugar, salt, fish sauce, and chicken broth to slow cooker. Stir to combine. Cover and cook on low for 5 to 6 hours, or on high for 2 to 3 hours.

4. Add the tofu, cover, and cook for 15 minutes on high.

5. Season with salt and gently stir in the sesame oil. Garnish with the scallions and serve with a side of rice.

> **CONTINUED**

Kimchi Stew

> CONTINUED

INGREDIENT TIP: Aged kimchi is best when making this meal, but if your kimchi hasn't reached that point yet, add 2 teaspoons of vinegar to the slow cooker. Not all kimchi is the same—it varies in saltiness, sweetness, and spiciness—so after cooking, taste your jjigae and add salt or sugar if needed.

OPTION TIP: Gochujang is a fermented red chili paste that is used in a lot of Korean cooking. If you want your stew spicier, add more gochujang.

Per Serving: Calories: 273; Total fat: 12g; Protein: 30g; Carbs: 10g; Fiber: 2g; Sugar: 5g; Sodium: 1,586mg

JAPAN

SHOYU PORK RAMEN

Prep time: 20 minutes, plus 1 hour to marinate

Cook time: 7 to 8 hours on low, 3 to 4 hours on high

Serves 5 or 6

Ramen is a hearty and magical noodle soup that can be labor-intensive and complicated. If you can, get the real deal at a ramen house and you'll taste what I mean. Unfortunately, I don't have the time or expertise to make ramen like that at home, so I leave that wisdom up to the professionals. Instead, I've found a method that uses a slow cooker to take out some of the work, while also stepping it up a notch from the instant ramen packets you get at the grocery store. This shoyu-based ramen will satisfy your ramen craving at home.

For the marinade

½ cup soy sauce

¼ cup mirin

¼ cup sake

1 tablespoon brown sugar

3 garlic cloves, smashed

2-inch piece fresh ginger, peeled and grated

1 tablespoon vegetable oil

½ teaspoon freshly ground black pepper

1½ to 2 pounds pork shoulder

To make the marinade

In a large bowl or resealable bag, combine the soy sauce, mirin, sake, brown sugar, garlic, ginger, oil, and pepper. Add the pork and turn to coat. Cover and marinate in the refrigerator for 1 hour or as long as overnight.

To make the soup

1. In a large pan, heat the vegetable oil over medium-high heat. Take the pork out of the marinade, then brown the pork on all sides in the pan, 3 to 5 minutes. Discard the marinade.

2. Transfer the pork to the slow cooker, then add the chicken broth, dashi stock, onion, garlic, and ginger.

3. Cover and cook on low for 7 to 8 hours, or on high for 3 to 4 hours.

4. Remove the pork, ginger, garlic, and onion from the slow cooker. Skim off any fats or solids with a sieve until the broth is clear. You can also strain the broth through a sieve into a large heatproof bowl, then pour it back into the slow cooker.

> **CONTINUED**

Shoyu Pork Ramen

> **CONTINUED**

For the soup

1 teaspoon vegetable oil

4 cups low-sodium
    chicken broth

4 cups dashi stock
    (2 teaspoons dashi
    powder dissolved in 4 cups
    hot water)

1 medium yellow onion,
    quartered

3 garlic cloves, smashed

2-inch piece fresh ginger,
    peeled and sliced

5 tablespoons soy sauce

1 tablespoon mirin

1 tablespoon sake

1 teaspoon sesame oil

1 pound ramen noodles

Scallions, both white and
    green parts thinly sliced,
    for serving

Shichimi (Japanese seven-
    spice blend), for serving

Corn kernels, for serving

Soft-boiled eggs, halved,
    for serving

Mung bean sprouts, blanched,
    for serving

Nori, for serving

5. Add the soy sauce, mirin, sake, and sesame oil to the slow cooker.

6. Cover and cook on high for 15 minutes.

7. Meanwhile, cut the pork into thin slices.

8. In a large pot, cook the ramen noodles according to package instructions. Drain the noodles and divide among bowls.

9. Ladle the broth over the noodles and top with a few slices of pork. Add scallions, shichimi, corn, 1 or 2 soft-boiled egg halves, mung bean sprouts, and nori as desired, and serve.

SUBSTITUTION TIP: Dashi powder can be purchased in an Asian grocery store or online. If you cannot find it, just substitute more chicken broth for the dashi stock.

OPTION TIP: For an even simpler preparation, just season the pork with salt and refrigerate it at least 1 hour or as long as overnight instead of marinating the meat.

PREP IT RIGHT: Prepare as many toppings as you like beforehand so that you can quickly assemble your ramen when serving.

Per Serving: Calories: 776; Total fat: 43g; Protein: 42g; Carbs: 53g; Fiber: 4g; Sugar: 10g; Sodium: 1,891mg

LAKSA NOODLE SOUP

Prep time: **15 minutes**

Cook time: **5 to 6 hours on low, 3 to 4 hours on high**

Serves **6**

INDONESIA,
MALAYSIA,
SINGAPORE

The first time I had Laksa, I was in Sydney. Australia has a large Southeast Asian immigrant population, so it was easy to find this spicy, rich, coconut-flavored soup. I fell in love with this noodle dish and was so disappointed when I could not find many restaurants that served it when I returned home. To make my own, I would set aside a weekend day to prepare the paste and cook the soup. We are using the shortcut method here by using laksa paste that you can purchase.

1 tablespoon vegetable oil

¾ cup laksa paste

1 to 1½ pounds boneless, skinless chicken thighs, cut into ½-inch slices

4 garlic cloves, minced

1 (13.5-ounce) can coconut milk

2 tablespoons fish sauce

6 cups water

12 to 15 medium shrimp, peeled and deveined

2 cups fried tofu puffs, cut diagonally in half

14 ounces rice noodles

Fresh cilantro, chopped, for garnish

Red chiles, thinly sliced, for garnish

Lime wedges, for garnish

1. In a small saucepan, heat the oil over medium heat.

2. Add the laksa paste and fry until it darkens, stirring constantly, about 5 minutes.

3. In the slow cooker, add the fried laksa paste, chicken, garlic, coconut milk, fish sauce, and water.

4. Cover and cook on low for 5 to 6 hours, or on high for 3 to 4 hours.

5. Add the shrimp and tofu puffs, cover, and cook on high for 10 more minutes.

6. Cook the noodles according to package instructions. Drain and rinse the noodles, and divide among bowls.

7. Ladle the laksa soup into the bowls and garnish with cilantro and red chiles. Serve with lime wedges on the side.

SUBSTITUTION TIP: You can find laksa paste in an Asian grocery store or online. But if you're having trouble finding it, you can use Thai red curry paste as a substitute.

Per Serving: Calories: 703 ; Total fat: 31g; Protein: 49g; Carbs: 54g; Fiber: 3g; Sugar: 3g; Sodium: 1,067mg

VIETNAMESE BEEF STEW

Prep time: **15 minutes**

Cook time: **6 to 7 hours on low, 3 to 4 hours on high**

Serves **6 or 7**

VIETNAM

I think slow cookers were made for stews like this one. *Bo Kho* is similar to a Western beef stew but with some beloved Asian ingredients. Star anise, lemongrass, and Chinese five-spice powder add layers that are oh-so aromatic and flavorful. You can serve this over a bowl of cooked rice noodles, but I am a fan of eating it with a slice of crusty French bread.

2 pounds beef chuck roast, cut into 1½- to 2-inch cubes

1 teaspoon salt

2 teaspoons Chinese five-spice powder

3 tablespoons vegetable oil, divided

3 garlic cloves, minced

1 medium yellow onion, finely diced, divided

2 tablespoons tomato paste

4 medium carrots, cut into 1- to 1½-inch pieces

2 stalks lemongrass, tough outer layers removed, bruised and cut into 3-inch sections

2 whole star anise

2 cups coconut water

3 cups water

Salt

Freshly ground black pepper

Chopped fresh cilantro, for garnish

1. In a large bowl, combine the beef, salt, and five-spice powder and mix well.

2. In a large pan, heat 2 tablespoons of oil over medium-high heat. Add the beef to the pan and brown on all sides, about 5 minutes.

3. Transfer the beef to the slow cooker and return the pan to the stove. Lower the heat to medium.

4. In the pan, add the remaining 1 tablespoon of oil, garlic, and most of the onion, reserving about ¼ cup of onion for garnish. Sauté until onion is soft, 3 to 5 minutes.

5. Add the tomato paste to the pan and cook until the tomato paste darkens, another 3 to 5 minutes. Turn off the heat and transfer the onion mixture to the slow cooker.

6. In the slow cooker, add the carrots, lemongrass, star anise, coconut water, and water.

7. Cover and cook on low for 6 to 7 hours, or on high for 3 to 4 hours.

8. Remove the lemongrass and star anise. Season the stew with salt and pepper.

9. Ladle into bowls and garnish with cilantro and the reserved onion. Serve with a side of warm French bread or over cooked rice noodles.

TIME-SAVING TIP: If you don't have time to brown the beef or sauté the garlic and onion first, just add all the ingredients to the slow cooker. Alternatively, you can cook the beef and the onion mixture the night before and store them separately in the fridge until you're ready to use the slow cooker.

Per Serving: Calories: 467; Total fat: 33g; Protein: 30g; Carbs: 10g; Fiber: 3g; Sugar: 6g; Sodium: 600mg

BEEF KARE RAISU FROM SCRATCH, PAGE 52

4

CURRIES

LAMB ROGAN JOSH 48

CHICKEN TIKKA MASALA 49

RED CHICKEN CURRY 51

BEEF KARE RAISU FROM SCRATCH 52

CHICKEN KARE RAISU 54

RED LENTIL CURRY 55

FILIPINO CHICKEN CURRY 56

PORK BELLY CURRY 57

CHICKEN DEVIL CURRY 59

BEEF RENDANG 61

KHMER CURRY 63

CHICKEN KURMA 64

Curry **is a difficult word for me to tackle.** Why? Because it became an umbrella term for a vast amount of dishes and spices from an area that is the most populated continent of the world. Am I totally guilty of using the term? Sure I am! I even use the "curry" spice blend you find in stores, the one most people generally think of when they hear the word *curry*. It's almost like using *Bolognese* as an umbrella term for every Italian pasta sauce. That would be weird, right? So yes, I warned you that this is a tricky one for me.

But let's at least understand that curry is not a single spice, nor does it have the same flavor profile between regions and countries. The texture of curry dishes can be dry or very saucy. Many South Asian curries use dry spice blends that linger on the palate, while curries of Southeast Asia tend to use fresh herbs that are ground into a paste. You'll see coconut milk being used in both of those regions, but you won't find it much (if at all) in East Asian curries. What you will find in all regions are "curries" that are delicious and unique. They are warming and satisfying dishes that pair well with rice or bread.

LAMB ROGAN JOSH

Prep time: 15 minutes

Cook time: 6 to 7 hours on low, 3 to 4 hours on high

Serves 6 or 7

INDIA

There are a few variations of Rogan Josh, but the deep red color comes from Kashmiri chiles. Finding Kashmiri chiles can be hit or miss, so here's a variation using paprika and cayenne pepper. Some recipes call for onions, garlic, and tomatoes. I've omitted all of these here since Kashmiri Brahmins avoid onion and garlic, and tomatoes are a Western influence. However, those adaptations are also good, so you can start with this base and build your own version.

3 tablespoons vegetable oil

2 teaspoons cumin seeds

1 cinnamon stick

5 cardamom pods

4 whole cloves

1 teaspoon whole black peppercorns

2 bay leaves

2-inch piece fresh ginger, peeled and minced

2 to 3 pounds lamb shoulder or boneless leg of lamb, cut into large cubes

4 teaspoons paprika

1 teaspoon ground cayenne pepper

½ cup water

⅓ cup plain whole-milk yogurt

1 teaspoon garam masala

Salt

1. In a large pan, heat the vegetable oil over medium-high heat. Add the cumin seeds, cinnamon, cardamom pods, cloves, peppercorns, and bay leaves, and fry until fragrant, about 2 minutes.

2. Add the ginger and fry for another 2 minutes.

3. Add the lamb and sear for 3 to 5 minutes.

4. Transfer the lamb and fried spices to the slow cooker.

5. In a small bowl, mix the paprika, cayenne, and water together. Pour the mixture into the slow cooker and stir to combine.

6. Cover and cook on low for 6 to 7 hours, or on high for 3 to 4 hours.

7. Stir in the yogurt a spoonful at a time and mix well. Cover and cook on high for another 15 minutes.

8. Add the garam masala and season with salt. Serve with rice.

PREP IT RIGHT: Speed up prep time in the morning by doing steps 1 to 3 the night before.

Per Serving: Calories: 384; Total fat: 21g; Protein: 46g; Carbs: 2g; Fiber: 1g; Sugar: 1g; Sodium: 196mg

CHICKEN TIKKA MASALA

Prep time: 15 minutes, plus 30 minutes to marinate

Cook time: 6 hours on low, 3 hours on high

Serves 6 or 7

INDIA

The first time I had Chicken Tikka Masala was over 20 years ago. It was creamy, had a delicious tomato base flavor, and also had a tiny bit of spiciness. Over the years, though, I've noticed it getting a little less hot. Either that or my tolerance for spice has gone to new heights. I omit the cayenne pepper when I cook this meal for those who want the curry flavor but not the heat. This popular dish is traditionally made by grilling the chicken first, then tossing it in the sauce at the end. But I've simplified it here by cooking the chicken in the slow cooker with the other ingredients.

For the marinade

1 cup plain whole-milk
    Greek yogurt
3 garlic cloves, minced
2 teaspoons peeled, minced
    fresh ginger
1 teaspoon ground coriander
1 teaspoon salt
1 teaspoon garam masala
Juice of 1 lemon
2 pounds skinless, boneless
    chicken thighs, cut into
    large cubes

To make the marinade

1. In a large bowl, combine the yogurt, garlic, ginger, coriander, salt, garam masala, and lemon juice, and mix well.

2. Add the chicken and toss to coat. Cover and marinate for at least 30 minutes, or refrigerate overnight.

To make the curry

1. In a medium pan, heat the vegetable oil over medium-high heat, and add the onion, ginger, and garlic. Sauté until the onion is soft and lightly brown, about 5 minutes. Transfer to the slow cooker.

2. In a blender combine the tomatoes and tomato paste, and process until smooth. Transfer to the slow cooker.

3. In the slow cooker, add the garam masala, cayenne pepper, paprika, turmeric, cumin, salt, and marinated chicken.

> **CONTINUED**

Chicken Tikka Masala

> **CONTINUED**

For the curry

1 tablespoon vegetable oil

1 large onion, finely diced

2 teaspoons peeled, minced
fresh ginger

1 tablespoon minced garlic

4 large tomatoes, quartered

2 tablespoons tomato paste

2 teaspoons garam masala

1 to 2 teaspoons
cayenne pepper

2 teaspoons paprika

½ teaspoon ground turmeric

2 teaspoons ground cumin

1 teaspoon salt

½ cup plain whole-milk
Greek yogurt

2 teaspoons sugar

Salt

Minced fresh cilantro,
for garnish

4. Cover and cook on low for 6 hours, or on high for 3 hours.

5. When the cooking is complete, stir in the yogurt and sugar. Season with salt. Garnish with fresh cilantro and serve with a side of rice.

SUBSTITUTION TIP: If you want to skip blending the tomatoes, you can use 4 cups canned puréed tomatoes instead. Just adjust the sugar (you may have to eliminate it altogether), since some canned tomatoes contain added sugar.

OPTION TIP: If you feel up to it, you can cook the marinated chicken in the oven, or grill until cooked through, and toss it in the sauce 15 minutes before the end of the cooking time.

Per Serving: Calories: 265; Total fat: 8g; Protein: 36g; Carbs: 12g; Fiber: 3g; Sugar: 7g; Sodium: 847mg

THAILAND

RED CHICKEN CURRY

Prep time: 15 minutes

Cook time: 5 hours on low, 2 to 3 hours on high

Serves 6

Kaeng Phed Kai is a popular Thai curry that is a winner among friends and family. It's slightly spicy, salty, tangy, creamy, and super satisfying. The vegetables I use here are suggestions; you can swap them out for others. Cook most of the ingredients in the slow cooker and let it do what it does best—merge all the flavors together. Then add the coconut milk at the end for a rich, creamy, and delicious curry.

Cooking spray

1½ pounds boneless, skinless chicken thighs, cut into ½-inch strips

4 to 5 Thai or Japanese eggplant, cut into wedges

3 tablespoons Thai red curry paste

3 tablespoons fish sauce

1 cup low-sodium chicken broth

1½ tablespoons palm sugar or coconut sugar

6 kaffir lime leaves

3 cups coconut milk

1 cup Thai basil leaves

1 cup fresh green beans, cut into 1-inch lengths

1 red bell pepper, seeded and thinly sliced

Fresh cilantro, for garnish

1. Spray the slow cooker lightly with cooking spray.

2. In the slow cooker, place the chicken on the bottom, then add the eggplant on top of the chicken.

3. In a small bowl, whisk together the curry paste, fish sauce, and broth, then transfer the mixture to the slow cooker. Add the palm sugar and kaffir leaves.

4. Cover and cook on low for 5 hours, or on high for 2 to 3 hours.

5. Add the coconut milk, basil, green beans, and bell pepper.

6. Cover and cook on high for 15 to 20 minutes.

7. Garnish with cilantro and serve with a side of jasmine rice.

INGREDIENT TIP: Palm sugar comes in hard discs. Remember to melt them before measuring and cooking.

SUBSTITUTION TIP: If you cannot find kaffir lime leaves, use lime peels. If you cannot find palm or coconut sugar, use brown sugar.

Per Serving: Calories: 579; Total fat: 36g; Protein: 31g; Carbs: 41g; Fiber: 19g; Sugar: 21g; Sodium: 1,225mg

JAPAN

BEEF KARE RAISU FROM SCRATCH

Prep time: **20 minutes**

Cook time: **5 to 6 hours on low, 2 to 3 hours on high**

Serves **6**

Many recipes call for store-bought curry blocks, but if you want to have some control over the roux ingredients and avoid the preservatives and MSG, making Japanese curry from scratch is a cinch. Just making the roux in a saucepan usually takes 30 minutes, but you can do all the prep for this recipe in less time than that. I use beef in this recipe, but you can easily substitute chicken or pork, or omit the meat altogether.

6 tablespoons all-purpose flour

2 tablespoons S&B curry powder

2 teaspoons salt

½ teaspoon ground cayenne pepper (optional)

1 to 1½ pounds beef stew meat, cut into ½- to 1-inch pieces

2 tablespoons vegetable oil

3 tablespoons butter

1 tablespoon ketchup

1 tablespoon tonkatsu sauce or Worcestershire sauce

4 cups low-sodium chicken broth

2 medium Yukon gold potatoes, cut into ½-inch cubes

3 medium carrots, cut into ½-inch cubes

1 medium yellow onion, diced

¼ cup frozen peas (optional)

¼ cup frozen or canned corn kernels (optional)

2 tablespoons cornstarch

¼ cup water

1. In a large bowl or resealable bag, combine the flour, curry powder, salt, and cayenne, if using. Add the beef to the flour mixture and stir to coat.

2. In a large pan, heat the oil over medium-high heat. Knock off the excess flour mixture from the beef and, reserving the flour mixture, place the beef in the pan and brown it on all sides. Transfer the browned meat to the slow cooker.

3. Adjust the heat to medium-low and add the butter. Once the butter is melted, add the reserved flour mixture, ketchup, and tonkatsu sauce, and cook for 5 minutes, stirring regularly.

4. Add the broth to the pan and raise the heat to medium-high. Cook for 2 minutes. Turn the heat off and transfer the sauce to the slow cooker.

5. In the slow cooker, add the potatoes, carrots, and onion.

6. Cover and cook on low for 5 to 6 hours, or on high for 2 to 3 hours.

7. Add the peas and/or corn kernels, if using.

8. In a small bowl, combine the cornstarch and water. Mix well, then pour into the slow cooker.

9. Cover and cook on high for 15 minutes. Once the sauce is thickened, stir and serve over rice.

SUBSTITUTION TIP: If you do not have S&B curry powder, you can use 1 tablespoon of any curry powder plus 1 tablespoon garam masala.

PREP IT RIGHT: Most of the prep time is from chopping vegetables. You can do all this prep beforehand and store the veggies in the fridge until you are ready to cook.

DIET TIP: Tonkatsu sauce usually has gluten in it, so use Worcestershire sauce for a gluten-free option.

Per Serving: Calories: 375; Total fat: 17g; Protein: 29g; Carbs: 26g; Fiber: 3g; Sugar: 4g; Sodium: 1,010mg

CHICKEN KARE RAISU

JAPAN

Prep time: **15 minutes**

Cook time: **6 to 8 hours on low, 3 to 4 hours on high**

Serves **6 or 7**

I feel like this dish is my "Get Out of Jail Free" card. I throw everything in the slow cooker and have a delicious curry the entire family loves. This version uses the curry roux blocks available at most grocery stories in the Asian food aisle. You can use any Japanese curry brand, but I often see the S&B Golden Curry box. If you prefer, you can make the roux yourself (see Beef Kare Raisu from Scratch, page 52).

Cooking spray

2 pounds boneless, skinless chicken thighs, cut into 1-inch cubes

1 large yellow onion, diced

4 to 5 medium carrots, cut into ½-inch lengths

2 to 3 medium Yukon gold potatoes, cut into ½-inch cubes

1 (8.4-ounce) package S&B Golden Curry sauce mix or other Japanese curry sauce blocks

5 cups water

¼ cup frozen peas (optional)

¼ cup frozen or canned corn kernels (optional)

1. Spray the slow cooker lightly with cooking spray.

2. In the slow cooker, in this order, layer the chicken, onion, carrots, potatoes, and curry blocks. Add the water.

3. Cover and cook on low for 6 to 8 hours, or on high for 3 to 4 hours.

4. Add the peas and/or corn, if using, and cover and cook on high for another 5 to 10 minutes.

5. Stir the curry, making sure all roux blocks have dissolved and combined. Serve over short-grain rice.

DIET TIP: Make the dish vegan by leaving out the chicken and using 6 cups water.

Per Serving: Calories: 290; Total fat: 7g; Protein: 31g; Carbs: 23g; Fiber: 4g; Sugar: 4g; Sodium: 301mg

RED LENTIL CURRY

Prep time: 15 minutes

Cook time: 4 hours on low, 2 hours on high

Serves 6

SRI LANKA

This red lentil curry (*Parippu*) is hearty and aromatic and has a nice heat from the chiles. Serve with a side of rice and you have a complete protein-packed meal. If you'd like, add a little more liquid at the end to make it into a soup.

Cooking spray

3 tablespoons vegetable oil

1 medium onion, diced, divided

3 garlic cloves, minced

6 curry leaves

½ teaspoon mustard seeds (optional)

1 teaspoon red chili flakes

2 cups red lentils, rinsed and drained

1 to 2 green chiles, thinly sliced

½ teaspoon ground cayenne pepper

½ teaspoon ground turmeric

1 cinnamon stick

2 cardamom pods

2 whole cloves

4 cups hot water

½ cup coconut milk

Salt

1. Spray the slow cooker lightly with cooking spray.

2. In a medium pan, heat the oil over medium heat. Sauté half of the onion along with the garlic and curry leaves until the onion is tender, 3 to 4 minutes.

3. Add the mustard seeds, if using, and chili flakes. Sauté for another 2 to 3 minutes, or until the mustard seeds start to pop. Transfer the mixture to a bowl, cover, and set aside in the refrigerator.

4. In the slow cooker, add the lentils, the remaining half of the onion, green chiles, cayenne, turmeric, cinnamon stick, cardamom pods, cloves, and hot water. Stir gently to combine.

5. Cover and cook on low for 4 hours, or on high for 2 hours.

6. Add the coconut milk and the reserved onion mixture to the slow cooker and stir.

7. Cover and cook on high for 15 minutes.

8. Season with salt. Serve with a side of rice.

OPTION TIP: To make this dish into a soup, add more coconut milk and water in equal parts at the end, and add salt to taste.

SUBSTITUTION TIP: Although there is no great substitute for curry leaves, if you cannot find them, you can use 2 bay leaves instead.

Per Serving: Calories: 345; Total fat: 13g; Protein: 17g; Carbs: 42g; Fiber: 21g; Sugar: 3g; Sodium: 396mg

FILIPINO CHICKEN CURRY

Prep time: **15 minutes**

Cook time: **5 to 6 hours on low, 2½ to 3 hours on high**

Serves **6 or 7**

This Filipino Chicken Curry is an easy dish to prepare in the slow cooker. It is a hearty curry with a delicate sweetness from the sweet potatoes and coconut milk.

Cooking spray

1½ to 2 pounds boneless, skinless chicken thighs, cut into 2-inch cubes

1 large onion, diced

6 garlic cloves, minced

2 sweet potatoes, cut into 1-inch cubes

3 tablespoons curry powder

1 teaspoon salt, plus more if needed

2 tablespoons fish sauce, plus more if needed

1 cup water

1 red bell pepper, seeded and cut into ½-inch dice

1 green bell pepper, seeded and cut into ½-inch dice

3 cups coconut milk

1. Spray the slow cooker lightly with cooking spray.

2. In the slow cooker, in this order, layer the chicken, onion, garlic, and sweet potatoes.

3. In a small bowl, whisk together the curry powder, salt, fish sauce, and water. Pour the mixture into the slow cooker.

4. Cover and cook on low for 5 to 6 hours, or on high for 2½ to 3 hours.

5. Add the red bell pepper, green bell pepper, and coconut milk.

6. Cover and cook for 15 to 20 minutes on high.

7. Season with additional fish sauce or salt to taste. Serve with rice.

OPTION TIP: If you want to add a layer of flavor, sauté the onion and garlic in a pan with 1 tablespoon of vegetable oil until the onion is soft and lightly brown before adding them over the chicken.

Per Serving: Calories: 527; Total fat: 35g; Protein: 34g; Carbs: 24g; Fiber: 6g; Sugar: 8g; Sodium: 1,030mg

PORK BELLY CURRY

Prep time: **15 minutes**

Cook time: **5 to 6 hours on low, 2 to 3 hours on high**

Serves **4 or 5**

MYANMAR

Kaeng Hang Leh is not for the faint of heart. Pork belly is incredibly rich, so you've got that going on, plus all the layers of amazing flavors. You will have to make your own curry paste, but you can do it the night before. You'll have enough curry paste left over to freeze for another time.

For the curry paste

8 to 10 dried red chiles, seeded and covered in water until softened (about 20 minutes)

1-inch piece fresh galangal, peeled and sliced

2 teaspoons shrimp paste

3 stalks lemongrass, tender parts only, thinly sliced

1 teaspoon salt

2 shallots, sliced

3 tablespoons water, plus more if needed

To make the curry paste

In a blender combine the chiles, galangal, shrimp paste, lemongrass, salt, shallots, and water, and process into a fine paste. If you need more water, add 1 tablespoon at a time.

To make the curry

1. Spray the slow cooker lightly with cooking spray.

2. In a large pan, heat the oil over medium heat, and add half of the curry paste. (Reserve the other half for another use.) Fry the curry paste until it darkens a little and is fragrant, 3 to 5 minutes.

3. Add the pork to the pan, and sear for 1 to 2 minutes, until browned.

4. Transfer the pork and curry paste to the slow cooker, then add the curry powder, turmeric, dark soy sauce, fish sauce, and ginger.

5. In a small bowl, combine the palm sugar and water, then add the mixture to the slow cooker. Gently stir to combine all ingredients.

> **CONTINUED**

Pork Belly Curry

> **CONTINUED**

For the curry

Cooking spray

1 tablespoon vegetable oil

2 pounds skinless pork belly
   or pork shoulder, cut into
   1½-inch cubes

1 teaspoon curry powder

½ teaspoon ground turmeric

2 tablespoons dark soy sauce

3 tablespoons fish sauce

2-inch piece fresh ginger,
   peeled and julienned

3 tablespoons palm sugar

½ cup water

¼ cup thinly sliced shallots

¼ cup pickled garlic

3 tablespoons tamarind paste

Salt

Fried shallots, for garnish

Fresh cilantro, for garnish

6. Cover and cook on low for 5 to 6 hours, or on high for
   2 to 3 hours.

7. Stir in the shallots, pickled garlic, and tamarind paste.
   Cover and cook on high for 15 minutes.

8. Season with salt and garnish with fried shallots and
   cilantro. Serve with short-grain rice.

SUBSTITUTION TIP: Tamarind has tangy and sour flavors that are
difficult to replicate. But if you cannot find tamarind paste, you
can use lime juice.

PREP IT RIGHT: The curry paste can be made ahead and stored in
a tightly sealed container in the refrigerator for 2 weeks, or in
the freezer for 3 months.

Per Serving: Calories: 339; Total fat: 13g; Protein: 45g; Carbs: 10g;
Fiber: 1g; Sugar: 7g; Sodium: 2,765mg

CHICKEN DEVIL CURRY

Prep time: 20 minutes

Cook time: 5 hours on low, 2½ to 3 hours on high

Serves 6 or 7

SINGAPORE

It can be difficult to find a lot of premade curry pastes at the grocery store. Luckily, making your own is not difficult; all it requires is a blender and about 5 minutes of your time. *Curry Debal* is a classic dish from Singapore comes from the Portuguese Eurasian community, and the name says it all—it's HOT—and it's supposed to be that way. It has a hint of tang and a slight sweetness to it, too. Once, I purchased red chiles that were not that spicy, so taste a dab of the curry paste before moving on. If you like more heat, use more chiles.

For the curry paste

20 to 30 dried red chiles, halved lengthwise and covered in water until softened (about 20 minutes)

2 red jalapeños, stemmed

2-inch piece fresh galangal, peeled and sliced

6 garlic cloves

1 large onion, quartered

3 tablespoons water, plus more if needed

To make the curry paste

In a blender combine the chiles, jalapeños, galangal, garlic, onion, and water, and process into a fine paste. If you need more water, add 1 tablespoon at a time.

To make the curry

1. Spray the slow cooker lightly with cooking spray.

2. In a medium pan, heat the oil over medium-high heat. Sauté the onion until soft, about 3 minutes. Add the tomatoes and cook for another 3 minutes, until the tomatoes are heated through and softened.

3. Add the curry paste to the pan and fry until the paste darkens a little and is fragrant, about 5 minutes.

> CONTINUED

Chicken Devil Curry

> **CONTINUED**

For the curry

Cooking spray

2 tablespoons vegetable oil

1 large onion, cut into
¼-inch slices

2 tomatoes, cut into
½-inch dice

1½ to 2 pounds boneless,
skinless chicken thighs, cut
into 2-inch cubes

½ cup chicken broth or water

1 tablespoon mustard seeds,
lightly crushed

2 teaspoons sugar, plus more
if needed

1 teaspoon salt, plus more
if needed

½ teaspoon ground turmeric

3 medium Yukon potatoes,
cut into 1-inch cubes
(optional)

2 cups cooked smoked
sausage, cut into bite-
size pieces

2 cups roughly
chopped cabbage

2 tablespoons white vinegar

4. In the slow cooker, add the chicken, curry paste, broth, mustard seeds, sugar, salt, turmeric, and potatoes, if using, and stir until combined.

5. Cover and cook on low for 5 to 6 hours, or on high for 2½ to 3 hours.

6. Add the sausage and cabbage and mix well. Cover and cook on high for another 15 minutes.

7. Stir in the vinegar and season with additional salt and sugar to taste. Serve with rice.

PREP IT RIGHT: The curry paste can be made up to a few days ahead and stored in a tightly sealed container in the refrigerator. For a larger batch, you can double the recipe and freeze the paste for up to 3 months.

Per Serving: Calories: 456; Total fat: 21g; Protein: 37g; Carbs: 30g; Fiber: 6g; Sugar: 8g; Sodium: 848mg

BEEF RENDANG

Prep time: 20 minutes

Cook time: 7 to 8 hours on low, 3½ to 4 hours on high

Serves 4 or 5

MALAYSIA
SINGAPORE

A coconut beef curry, Beef Rendang is usually cooked on a stove over a low heat for many hours until the sauce is almost dried out. Instead of worrying and checking on the beef to make sure it doesn't burn, using the slow cooker eliminates that stress.

For the rendang paste

12 dried red chiles, covered in water until softened (about 20 minutes)

6 garlic cloves

1-inch piece fresh galangal, peeled and sliced

1-inch piece fresh ginger, peeled and sliced

3 stalks lemongrass, white part only

1 small onion, quartered

3 tablespoons water, plus more if needed

To make the rendang paste

In a blender jar, combine the chiles, garlic, galangal, ginger, lemongrass, onion, and water, and process into a fine paste. If you need more water, add 1 tablespoon at a time.

To make the curry

1. Spray the slow cooker lightly with cooking spray.

2. In a large pan, heat the oil over medium heat. Add the rendang paste to the pan and cook until it turns a shade darker, 2 to 3 minutes.

3. Add the cinnamon stick, cloves, star anise, and cardamom pods, and fry for 2 to 3 minutes, until fragrant.

4. Add the brisket to the pan, brown on all sides, and coat with the paste. Transfer the brisket to the slow cooker.

> **CONTINUED**

Beef Rendang

> **CONTINUED**

For the curry

Cooking spray

3 tablespoons vegetable oil

1 cinnamon stick

4 whole cloves

3 whole star anise

3 cardamom pods

2 pounds brisket, cut into
2-inch cubes

1 tablespoon palm sugar, plus
more if needed

1 teaspoon salt, plus more
if needed

2 tablespoons tamarind paste

6 kaffir lime leaves or 6 large
pieces lime peel

⅓ cup unsweetened
toasted coconut

1 (13.5-ounce) can
coconut milk

2 tablespoons cornstarch

2 tablespoons cold water

5. In the slow cooker, add the palm sugar, salt, tamarind paste, kaffir leaves, toasted coconut, and coconut milk.

6. Cover and cook on low 7 to 8 hours, or on high for 3½ to 4 hours.

7. In a small bowl, whisk together the cornstarch and cold water. Pour the mixture into the slow cooker and stir.

8. Cover and cook on high for 15 minutes, or until the sauce thickens. Season with additional salt and sugar, if desired.

9. Using a slotted spoon, transfer the meat to a serving bowl. Serve with a side of rice.

TIME-SAVING TIP: Premade rendang curry paste can be purchased at an Asian grocery store or online if you want to bypass making your own.

Per Serving: Calories: 812; Total fat: 59g; Protein: 52g; Carbs: 23g; Fiber: 6g; Sugar: 10g; Sodium: 614mg

KHMER CURRY

Prep time: 20 minutes

Cook time: 5 to 6 hours on low, 2½ to 3 hours on high

Serves 6

CAMBODIA

Traditionally, *kroeung* curry paste is made by grinding up ingredients with a mortar and pestle (as with most curry pastes), and this yellow kroeung gets its color from turmeric. Although a mortar and pestle are the best tools to release the oils and use less water, a blender is a fast alternative. I've used chicken and pork for this curry, and it pairs well with pumpkin.

For the kroeung

2-inch piece fresh galangal, peeled and sliced

3 stalks lemongrass, tender parts only, sliced

4 kaffir lime leaves

½ teaspoon ground turmeric

8 garlic cloves

2 shallots, peeled

3 tablespoons water

For the curry

Cooking spray

1½ pounds chicken thighs or pork shoulder

3 cups peeled and diced sugar pumpkin (if not available use butternut squash or kabocha)

1 cup low-sodium chicken broth or water

2 tablespoons fish sauce

1 teaspoon prahok (fermented fish paste) or shrimp paste

1 tablespoon palm sugar

3 cups coconut milk

To make the kroeung

In a blender combine the galangal, lemongrass, kaffir leaves, turmeric, garlic, shallots, and water. Process into a fine paste.

To make the curry

1. Spray the slow cooker lightly with cooking spray.

2. In a medium pan, heat the oil over medium-high heat. Fry the kroeung until the paste darkens a little and is fragrant, 3 to 5 minutes.

3. In the slow cooker, add the chicken or pork, kroeung, pumpkin, broth, fish sauce, prahok, and palm sugar, and mix to combine.

4. Cover and cook on low for 5 to 6 hours, or on high for 2½ to 3 hours.

5. Stir in the coconut milk, cover, and cook on high for 15 more minutes. Serve with a side of rice.

OPTION TIP: You can use shrimp in this dish instead of chicken or pork. Add it at the end with the coconut milk and cook on high for 15 minutes.

PREP IT RIGHT: The kroeung can be blended and fried a few days ahead and stored in a tightly sealed container in the refrigerator.

Per Serving: Calories: 548; Total fat: 46g; Protein: 24g; Carbs: 13g; Fiber: 3g; Sugar: 6g; Sodium: 655mg

CHICKEN KURMA

Prep time: 20 minutes

Cook time: 5 hours on low, 2½ to 3 hours on high

Serves 6

MALAYSIA
SINGAPORE

Originally from India, *Ayam Kurmah* is a Malaysian and Singaporean interpretation of korma. Coconut milk is used in place of yogurt, and you also get a nutty flavor from the ground almonds. This is a mild and hearty curry that is rich and creamy. If you prefer, you can purchase premade korma paste at an Asian grocery store or online.

For the curry paste

8 garlic cloves, finely minced

2 tablespoons ground coriander

2 teaspoons ground fennel

1 tablespoon ground cumin

1 teaspoon ground white pepper

3 tablespoons water

To make the curry paste

In a small bowl, combine the garlic, coriander, fennel, cumin, white pepper, and water, and stir until it forms a paste.

To make the curry

1. Spray the slow cooker lightly with cooking spray.

2. In a medium pan, heat the oil over medium heat. Sauté the onion and ginger, cooking until tender, about 3 minutes.

3. Add the cardamom pods, cinnamon stick, and cloves, and cook for another 5 minutes, until fragrant.

4. Add the spice paste to the pan and heat for another 5 minutes, stirring constantly. Transfer to the slow cooker.

5. In the slow cooker, add the chicken, turmeric, salt, sugar, potatoes, and water, and mix well.

For the curry

Cooking spray

2 tablespoons vegetable oil

1 medium onion, sliced

1 tablespoon peeled, finely minced fresh ginger

4 cardamom pods

1 cinnamon stick

5 whole cloves

8 boneless, skinless chicken thighs, cut into 2-inch chunks

½ teaspoon ground turmeric

2 teaspoons salt, plus more if needed

2 teaspoons sugar

2 Yukon gold potatoes, cut into 1-inch cubes

½ cup water

¼ cup ground almonds

3 cups coconut milk

Juice of 1 lime

Fried shallots, for garnish

Fresh cilantro, for garnish

6. Cover and cook on low for 5 hours or on high for 2½ to 3 hours.

7. In a small bowl, mix the ground almonds, coconut milk, and lime juice. Add the mixture to slow cooker, cover, and cook on high for 15 more minutes.

8. Season with additional salt. Garnish with fried shallots and fresh cilantro. Serve with a side of rice.

TIME-SAVING TIP: You can purchase premade korma curry paste at an Asian grocery store or online instead of making your own.

Per Serving: Calories: 590; Total fat: 42g; Protein: 35g; Carbs: 25g; Fiber: 6g; Sugar: 7g; Sodium: 935mg

SPICED CAULIFLOWER & POTATOES, PAGE 70

5

VEGETABLES & TOFU

MAPO TOFU 68

SPICED CAULIFLOWER & POTATOES 70

EGGPLANT & THAI BASIL 71

SIMMERED PUMPKIN 72

SOY SILKEN TOFU 73

SPICED POTATOES 74

STEAMED EGG WITH MUSHROOM & ASPARAGUS 75

SPICY CHICKPEAS & POTATOES 77

EGGPLANT SAMBAL 78

INDONESIAN BRAISED TOFU 79

One of my favorite challenges is changing someone's opinion about an ingredient or introducing them to a new one. Someone once told me that they didn't like tofu, and I replied, "Well, I guess that's what I'm making for dinner tonight!" It's happened over and over, with things like Brussels sprouts, eggplant, and mushrooms.

It blows my mind when I think about how many different varieties of vegetables are available and used in Asia. All kinds of leafy greens, root and bulb vegetables, stems—the list goes on. While many Asian vegetable dishes are traditionally prepared quickly, there are some that work well in the slow cooker. For instance, vegetables like eggplant are sponges that soak up oil when fried in a pan. Instead, use the slow cooker and your eggplant will soak up flavors from the seasonings without the added oil.

MAPO TOFU

Prep time: **15 minutes**

Cook time: **3 to 4 hours on low, 1½ to 2 hours on high**

Serves **6**

CHINA

There are so many variations of Mapo Tofu. Traditionally, it's made with minced beef or pork, but this is a vegan version made with dried shiitake mushrooms. Mapo Tofu is one of my favorite dishes, and I cannot eat it without ground Sichuan peppercorns. They give a tingling, mouth-numbing sensation and are usually found in Chinese five-spice powder. They are not spicy on their own, so you can thank the chiles in the *doubanjiang* for the heat. If you want more heat, you can add red pepper flakes in step 4 to kick it up a notch.

Cooking spray

2 (14-ounce) packages firm tofu, drained and cut into 1-inch cubes

2 tablespoons vegetable oil

5 garlic cloves, minced

2 teaspoons peeled, minced fresh ginger

6 to 8 dried shiitake mushrooms, rehydrated and thinly sliced

3 tablespoons low-sodium soy sauce

1 teaspoon sesame oil

2 tablespoons douchi (fermented black beans)

2 tablespoons doubanjiang (Sichuan bean paste)

¼ cup water, plus 3 tablespoons

2 tablespoons potato starch or cornstarch

1 teaspoon ground Sichuan pepper (optional)

2 scallions, both white and green parts thinly sliced, for garnish

1. Spray the slow cooker lightly with cooking spray.

2. In the slow cooker, arrange the tofu.

3. In a medium pan, heat the oil over medium heat. Add the garlic, ginger, and mushrooms, and sauté until fragrant, about 3 minutes.

4. Add the soy sauce, sesame oil, douchi, and doubanjiang, and cook for another 3 minutes, until just slightly thickened. Transfer the sauce to the slow cooker along with ¼ cup of water.

5. Cover and cook on low for 3 to 4 hours, or on high for 1½ to 2 hours.

6. In a small bowl, mix the potato starch and the remaining 3 tablespoons of water together. Pour the mixture into the slow cooker and carefully stir the ingredients together.

7. Cover and cook on high for 15 minutes.

8. Once the sauce has thickened, sprinkle the tofu with the ground Sichuan pepper, if using, and garnish with the scallions. Serve with a side of rice.

INGREDIENT TIP: Regular or firm tofu is easier to handle and cook with, but I like using soft tofu. It's not as soft as silken, but be careful when stirring.

OPTION TIP: You can replace the mushrooms with ground beef in this recipe if you'd like to add meat to this dish.

Per Serving: Calories: 253; Total fat: 16g; Protein: 15g; Carbs: 16g; Fiber: 4g; Sugar: 3g; Sodium: 798mg

INDIA

SPICED CAULIFLOWER & POTATOES

Prep time: **15 minutes**

Cook time: **3 to 4 hours on low, 2 hours on high**

Serves **6**

The flavors of all the spices make *Aloo Gobi* an exciting dish. The cauliflower and potatoes are substantial enough to stand on their own, but it's so good to have this dish with a side of rice or naan. If you're not into spicy food, you can eliminate the green chiles and cayenne pepper.

3 tablespoons vegetable oil, divided

1 head cauliflower, cored and cut into small florets

3 medium Yukon gold potatoes, cut into 1½-inch cubes

1 onion, finely diced

3 teaspoons peeled, grated fresh ginger

3 garlic cloves, finely minced

2 tomatoes, diced

2 green chiles, diced (seed them first for less heat)

2 teaspoons cumin seeds

1 teaspoon ground cayenne pepper

1 teaspoon ground turmeric

2 teaspoons salt, plus more if needed

2 teaspoons garam masala

¼ cup water

¼ cup chopped fresh cilantro

1. Coat the bottom and sides of the slow cooker with 1 tablespoon of oil.

2. Add the cauliflower, potatoes, and onion.

3. In a bowl, mix the remaining 2 tablespoons of oil, ginger, garlic, tomatoes, chiles, cumin, cayenne, turmeric, salt, and garam masala. Coat the potatoes and cauliflower evenly with the mixture, then add the water.

4. Cover and cook on low for 3 to 4 hours, or on high for 2 hours.

5. Season with additional salt and garnish with cilantro. Serve with a side of rice.

OPTION TIP: To add a bit more flavor, first sauté the onion, ginger, garlic, and cumin seeds in a pan with the vegetable oil. In a bowl, mix with the tomatoes, chiles, cayenne, turmeric, salt, and garam masala. Spray the slow cooker lightly with cooking spray instead of coating with oil. Add the cauliflower and potatoes, then coat them evenly with the tomato mixture and proceed with the recipe.

TIME-SAVING TIP: You can use canned diced tomatoes. Just substitute 2 (8-ounce) cans diced tomatoes for the fresh tomatoes and water.

Per Serving: Calories: 174; Total fat: 7g; Protein: 4g; Carbs: 25g; Fiber: 6g; Sugar: 5g; Sodium: 814mg

EGGPLANT & THAI BASIL

Prep time: 15 minutes

Cook time: 3 to 4 hours on low, 1½ to 2 hours on high

Serves 6 or 7

THAILAND

Chinese and Japanese eggplants are thinner and have fewer seeds compared with the Italian eggplants that we commonly see in supermarkets. Their skin is also thinner, and they have a more delicate flavor that is slightly less bitter. Sometimes it can be difficult to differentiate between the two Asian eggplants. Chinese eggplant is longer and can be more lavender in color, while Japanese eggplant is shorter with a dark purple hue. Nevertheless, both are delicious in *Pad Ma Kuer,* which is typically stir-fried and prepared with minced pork, but oil and pork were omitted here to achieve a lighter dish.

Cooking spray

2 pounds Chinese or
   Japanese eggplant, cut
   into 1-inch-thick rounds

6 garlic cloves, minced

2 to 3 Thai bird's eye chiles,
   julienned (optional)

½ cup oyster sauce

1 tablespoon brown sugar

1 tablespoon fish sauce

3 tablespoons soy sauce

2 tablespoons cornstarch

¼ cup water, plus
   2 tablespoons cold water

1½ cup loosely packed Thai
   basil leaves

Fresh cilantro, for garnish

1. Spray the slow cooker lightly with cooking spray.

2. In the slow cooker, arrange the eggplant slices.

3. In a medium bowl, mix the garlic, chiles (if using), oyster sauce, brown sugar, fish sauce, soy sauce, and ¼ cup of water. Pour the mixture over the eggplant and mix together.

4. Cover and cook on low for 3 to 4 hours or on high for 1½ to 2 hours.

5. In a small bowl, mix the cornstarch and 2 tablespoons of cold water.

6. Pour the cornstarch mixture into the slow cooker and add the Thai basil leaves. Cover and cook on high for 15 minutes.

7. Once the sauce thickens, garnish with cilantro. Serve with a side of rice.

OPTION TIP: If you'd like to add more color to the eggplant, heat a dry nonstick pan over medium heat. Place a layer of eggplant in the pan until one side is lightly browned. Flip over and brown the other side, then transfer the eggplant to the slow cooker.

Per Serving: Calories: 67; Total fat: 0g; Protein: 3g; Carbs: 15g; Fiber: 6g; Sugar: 6g; Sodium: 833mg

SIMMERED PUMPKIN

Prep time: **20 minutes**

Cook time: **2 to 2½ hours on low**

Serves **5 or 6**

JAPAN

When making *Kabocha no Nimono*, most of the prep time goes into cutting the kabocha squash. Be careful, as the squash has a hard outer layer! Sometimes you can find kabocha already cut in half to save you time. You can eat the skin once the squash is cooked, so don't fret over peeling. Whenever I make this, I cook two layers (even though the broth doesn't reach the top layer), and store the top layer and leftover broth for a meal the next day. This squash is light, delicious, and traditionally served as a side dish. However, it's great on its own for breakfast or as a snack.

Cooking spray

1 to 2 whole kabocha squash,
 cut into large, even chunks

1 cup dashi broth (½ teaspoon
 dashi powder dissolved in
 1 cup hot water)

2 tablespoons brown sugar

2 tablespoons soy sauce

2 tablespoons sake

1. Spray the slow cooker lightly with cooking spray.

2. Place kabocha squash pieces skin-side down in a single layer in the slow cooker. If you want to cook additional squash to save for later, add another layer. The extra squash will still be infused with the aroma of the broth.

3. In a small bowl, whisk together the broth, brown sugar, soy sauce, and sake. Pour the broth mixture over the squash.

4. Cover and cook on low for 2 to 2½ hours. Serve.

PREP IT RIGHT: You can cut the squash ahead of time and store it in the fridge for up to 5 days until ready to use.

Per Serving: Calories: 96; Total fat: 0g; Protein: 2g; Carbs: 22g; Fiber: 3g; Sugar: 4g; Sodium: 367mg

SOY SILKEN TOFU

Prep time: 10 minutes

Cook time: 3 hours on low, 1 to 2 hours on high

Serves 6

KOREA

When I was a kid, my mom made a lot of *dubu ganjangjorim*. It uses the same sauce, but the tofu was sliced and panfried first. I've adapted this dish with *soondubu* (silken tofu) cooked in a slow cooker so that the flavors are absorbed by the tofu, instead of just being poured on top. The silky texture of the tofu combined with the sweet and salty flavor of the sauce is wonderful.

Cooking spray

2 (16-ounce) packages silken tofu, drained

¾ cup soy sauce

½ cup seasoned rice vinegar

5 garlic cloves, finely minced

6 scallions, both white and green parts thinly sliced, divided

1 tablespoon gochugaru (Korean red chili flakes)

1 tablespoon roasted sesame seeds

1 teaspoon sesame oil (optional)

1. Spray the slow cooker lightly with cooking spray.

2. In the slow cooker, carefully arrange the tofu in one layer. If it breaks apart, that's okay. You just want to keep it in large pieces.

3. In a medium bowl, mix together the soy sauce, vinegar, garlic, only the white and pale green parts of the scallions, gochugaru, and sesame seeds.

4. In a separate bowl, reserve ½ cup of soy sauce mixture and add the dark green parts of the scallions to it. Set aside in the fridge.

5. Pour the rest of the sauce over the tofu.

6. Cover and cook on low for 3 hours, or on high for 1 to 2 hours.

7. Using a large slotted spoon, carefully remove the tofu and transfer to a serving bowl or plate.

8. Spoon the reserved soy sauce mixture on top, and drizzle with the sesame oil, if using. Serve with a side of rice.

INGREDIENT TIP: Seasoned rice vinegar is made with sugar and salt, and contains less acidity than regular rice vinegar. You can use regular rice vinegar instead, but if you do, add 3 teaspoons sugar to your sauce.

Per Serving: Calories: 129; Total fat: 5g; Protein: 12g; Carbs: 10g; Fiber: 1g; Sugar: 4g; Sodium: 1,931mg

SPICED POTATOES

Prep time: 15 minutes

Cook time: 2½ to 3 hours on low, 1 to 2 hours on high

Serves 5 or 6

SRI LANKA

A popular dish in Sri Lanka, *Ala Thel Dala* is extremely flavorful, spicy, and peppery. You will find Maldive fish in a lot of Sri Lankan cuisine, but I've omitted it here for this vegetarian version. Thanks to the slow cooker, there's no need to boil the potatoes first. And while butter isn't common in Sri Lankan cuisine (which traditionally uses coconut oil), I've found that it works well for potatoes in the slow cooker.

Vegetable oil, for greasing, plus 1 tablespoon

2 pounds baby potatoes, halved

1 medium onion, thinly sliced

6 to 8 curry leaves

4 whole cloves

4 cardamom pods

1 cinnamon stick

½ teaspoon ground turmeric

2 to 3 teaspoons red pepper flakes

2 teaspoons freshly ground black pepper

1½ teaspoons salt, plus more if needed

3 tablespoons unsalted butter, melted

Juice of 1 lime

1. Lightly grease the slow cooker with oil, and add the potatoes.

2. In a medium pan, heat the remaining 1 tablespoon of oil over medium-high heat. Add the onion and sauté until tender, about 3 minutes.

3. Add the curry leaves, cloves, cardamom, and cinnamon stick, and cook until fragrant, about 3 minutes. Add the turmeric, red pepper flakes, and black pepper. Cook for a few more minutes, stirring regularly to combine the spices well. Transfer the mixture to the slow cooker and add the salt. Mix well.

4. Pour the butter over the top.

5. Cover and cook on low for 2½ to 3 hours, or on high for 1 to 2 hours.

6. Season with additional salt and the lime juice. Serve with a side of rice.

DIET TIP: If you'd like to make this dish vegan, substitute the butter with 2 tablespoons melted coconut oil.

Per Serving: Calories: 223; Total fat: 10g; Protein: 4g; Carbs: 31g; Fiber: 5g; Sugar: 3g; Sodium: 2,619mg

STEAMED EGG WITH MUSHROOM & ASPARAGUS

TAIWAN

Prep time: **15 minutes**

Cook time: **1½ hours on high**

Serves **6**

As with congee and jook, there are many countries that have their own version of steamed eggs. There's *gyeran-jjim, chawanmushi, zheng shui dan,* and here we have a Taiwanese version, *Chawanzheng.* This dish is incredibly silky, light, and savory. Before, I would make steamed eggs on the stove or in the oven and achieve mixed results. But the slow cooker has given me consistent success every time. You can also adapt the recipe by adding vegetables to your liking. I even sneak in shrimp and scallops all the time.

6 large eggs

3 cups dashi stock or low-sodium vegetable stock

3 shiitake mushrooms, thinly sliced

6 asparagus spears, trimmed and cut into 1½-inch lengths

2 scallions, both white and green parts thinly sliced, for garnish

Soy sauce

1. Place a trivet or rack in a 6-quart slow cooker and pour in enough hot water to reach the top of the trivet.

2. In a mixing bowl, crack the eggs and beat them gently so as not to incorporate too much air.

3. Slowly add the stock to the eggs while you continue to mix.

4. Strain the egg mixture through a fine-mesh sieve into a heatproof bowl. (The bowl needs to fit in the slow cooker. If your slow cooker is oval, use 2 smaller bowls if necessary.)

> **CONTINUED**

Steamed Egg with Mushroom & Asparagus

> CONTINUED

5. Using the back of a spoon, smooth any air bubbles on the surface, then carefully place the mushrooms and asparagus on top.

6. Cover the bowl tightly with plastic wrap before placing it in the slow cooker. This helps achieve a smooth surface.

7. Cover and cook on high for 1½ hours.

8. Garnish with the scallions. Season with soy sauce and serve with a side of rice.

INGREDIENT TIP: To make dashi stock out of dashi powder, dissolve 1½ teaspoons in 3 cups water.

OPTION TIP: I use a 2-to-1 egg-to-stock ratio here, and you can use that as a starting guide. Some people like more egg flavor and use less stock, and others like a smoother texture and use more stock.

TECHNIQUE TIP: You can use canning jar lids if you do not have a trivet or rack.

Per Serving: Calories: 90; Total fat: 5g; Protein: 8g; Carbs: 4g; Fiber: 1g; Sugar: 3g; Sodium: 142mg

SPICY CHICKPEAS & POTATOES

SRI LANKA

Prep time: 20 minutes

Cook time: 8 hours on high

Serves 6

Kadala is one of my favorite vegan dishes. It has so much flavor and is incredibly satisfying. Depending on how spicy you like your food, add as much or as little cayenne pepper as you want. Remember, the slow cooker intensifies chili powder, so a little goes a long way!

Cooking spray

2 medium tomatoes

2-inch piece fresh ginger, peeled and sliced

8 garlic cloves

1 to 2 teaspoons ground cayenne pepper

1 teaspoon ground turmeric

1 teaspoon salt, plus more if needed

3 cups dried chickpeas, drained and rinsed

3 medium Yukon gold potatoes, peeled and cut into 1-inch cubes

2 tablespoons vegetable oil

3 teaspoons cumin seeds

3 sprigs curry leaves

2 medium yellow onions, finely diced

6 cups water

1 teaspoon garam masala

Juice of 1 lemon

1. Spray the slow cooker lightly with cooking spray.

2. In a blender add the tomatoes, ginger, garlic, cayenne, turmeric, and salt, and process well.

3. In the slow cooker, add the chickpeas, tomato mixture, and potatoes.

4. In a medium pan, heat the oil over medium-high heat. Add the cumin seeds and curry leaves, and cook for 2 minutes, until the curry leaves begin to wilt and turn a glossy, darker shade of green.

5. Add the onions and sauté until tender and light brown, about 5 minutes. Transfer the mixture to the slow cooker and add the water.

6. Cover and cook on high for 7 to 8 hours.

7. Season with additional salt, sprinkle with the garam masala, and squeeze the lemon juice on top. Mix well. Serve with a side of basmati rice or naan.

INGREDIENT TIP: Curry leaves are not the same as curry powder. There's no great substitution for curry leaves, but if you have to, use 3 bay leaves.

Per Serving: Calories: 259; Total fat: 6g; Protein: 8g; Carbs: 45g; Fiber: 7g; Sugar: 3g; Sodium: 702mg

EGGPLANT SAMBAL

Prep time: 20 minutes

Cook time: 3 or 4 hours on low, 1½ to 2 hours on high

Serves 6

SINGAPORE

Eggplant soaks up oil like a sponge, so when it's panfried, you have to use a good amount of oil. The slow cooker allows for the oil to be cut down considerably for this Eggplant Sambal recipe. The sauce is spicy, a little tangy, and garlicky, with deep flavors of tomato and shrimp pastes. For a vegan option, see the Diet tip (below).

Cooking spray

1½ pounds Chinese or Japanese eggplant, cut into ½-inch-thick rounds

10 dried red chiles, covered in water until softened (about 20 minutes)

5 fresh red chiles, sliced

4 shallots

6 garlic cloves

3 tablespoons vegetable oil

½ cup tamarind water

2 teaspoons belacan (dried fermented shrimp paste)

2 tablespoons tomato paste

1 teaspoon salt

1. Spray the slow cooker lightly with cooking spray.

2. In the slow cooker, arrange the eggplant.

3. In a blender combine the rehydrated chiles, fresh chiles, shallots, and garlic, and process to a fine paste.

4. In a medium pan, heat the oil over medium heat. Transfer the spice paste to the pan and fry for 3 to 4 minutes, until fragrant.

5. Stir in the tamarind water, belacan, tomato paste, and salt, and mix well. Pour the sauce over the eggplant.

6. Cover and cook on low for 3 to 4 hours, or on high for 1½ to 2 hours.

7. Serve with a side of rice.

SUBSTITUTION TIP: If you can't find tamarind paste to make tamarind water (see Asian Pantry, page 154), replace the tamarind water with ½ cup lemon or lime juice.

DIET TIP: To make this dish vegan, you can use Golden Mountain sauce instead of belacan. It is saltier than regular soy sauce but not as salty as belacan; you may need to use 3 to 4 teaspoons. Or you can substitute the belacan with 1 tablespoon vegetarian oyster sauce.

Per Serving: Calories: 118; Total fat: 7g; Protein: 3g; Carbs: 12g; Fiber: 4g; Sugar: 5g; Sodium: 556mg

INDONESIAN BRAISED TOFU

INDONESIA

Prep time: 10 minutes

Cook time: 3 to 4 hours on low, 1½ to 2 hours on high

Serves 6

Tahu Bacem is usually cooked with tofu, spices, and coconut water until the liquid evaporates, and then is panfried. Since liquids do not evaporate in a slow cooker, I use coconut milk instead of coconut water for a more intense coconut flavor. To finish, fry the tofu with *kecap manis* in a pan until golden, and you will reward yourself with a sweet, sour, and tasty Indonesian tofu dish.

2 (14-ounce) packages firm tofu, drained

Cooking spray

3 cups coconut milk

3 tablespoons tamarind water (if not available, use ½ cup fresh lemon or lime juice)

½-inch piece fresh galangal, peeled and cut into thick slices

2 shallots, diced

4 garlic cloves, minced

3 bay leaves

3 tablespoons brown sugar

2 teaspoons ground coriander

2 teaspoons salt

2 tablespoons vegetable oil

3 tablespoons kecap manis (Indonesian sweet soy sauce)

1. In a strainer, weight the tofu with a plate to extract water from the tofu.

2. Spray the slow cooker lightly with cooking spray.

3. In a large bowl, mix together the coconut milk, tamarind water, galangal, shallots, garlic, bay leaves, brown sugar, coriander, and salt.

4. Cut the tofu into 1-by-2-inch rectangles about ¼ inch thick, and place in the slow cooker.

5. Pour the coconut milk mixture over the tofu, making sure the liquid reaches the top of the tofu.

6. Cover and cook on low for 3 to 4 hours, or on high for 1½ to 2 hours.

7. In a large pan, heat the oil over medium heat.

8. Using a slotted spoon, remove the tofu from the slow cooker, leaving behind most of the liquid, and transfer it to the pan. Drizzle the kecap manis over the tofu and fry until golden, flipping once, 2 to 3 minutes per side.

9. Transfer to a serving dish and serve with a side of rice.

Per Serving: Calories: 436; Total fat: 39g; Protein: 14g; Carbs: 15g; Fiber: 4g; Sugar: 9g; Sodium: 1,262mg

BURMESE CHILI CHICKEN, PAGE 97

6

CHICKEN

CHICKEN ADOBO 82

MALAYSIAN CHICKEN WINGS 83

CHINESE FIVE-SPICE WHOLE CHICKEN 84

THREE-CUP CHICKEN 86

BELACAN NOT-FRIED CHICKEN 88

GINGER CHICKEN 89

HAINANESE CHICKEN RICE 90

ROAST CHICKEN 92

SPICY LEMONGRASS CHICKEN 93

STEAMED CHICKEN IN COCONUT WATER 94

KERALA THATTUKADA CHICKEN 96

BURMESE CHILI CHICKEN 97

CHICKEN TERIYAKI 98

LAOTIAN CHICKEN WITH MUSHROOMS 99

Other than the recipes that use a whole chicken, there aren't any dishes that call for chicken breasts here. The other parts (thighs, legs, and wings) are best for the slow cooker. The result is juicy and tender chicken with tasty flavors. You'll notice that in a few recipes in this book, like Chicken Adobo, vinegar is added at the end of cooking. This is so the sour taste that vinegar gives does not get lost when cooked in the slow cooker.

Caramelization will add another layer of depth to your dish, so if you can, take the extra few minutes to brown your chicken in the oven or a pan. Your slow cooker will do the rest for you, and you can tackle these recipes with ease. If you do brown your chicken in the oven, make sure to keep an eye on it because it can take only a few minutes to brown.

CHICKEN ADOBO

Prep time: **10 minutes**

Cook time: **4 to 5 hours on low, 2 to 3 hours on high**

Serves **5 or 6**

PHILIPPINES

Although it is a simple process to make Chicken Adobo, the variations and ratios of ingredients are vast. The trick here for the slow cooker is to add a little bit of vinegar at the end of cooking. Browning the chicken either before or after cooking time is optional, but it really does help bring out a nice caramelized flavor. You can forgo browning the chicken if you're in a hurry. Serve this tangy and savory chicken with a side of rice.

Cooking spray
½ cup soy sauce
½ cup white vinegar, plus 1 to 2 tablespoons
5 garlic cloves, minced
1 tablespoon dark brown sugar
2 teaspoons whole black peppercorns
4 bay leaves
1 tablespoon vegetable oil, for browning (optional)
3 to 4 pounds bone-in chicken thighs or drumsticks, with skin

1. Spray the slow cooker lightly with cooking spray.

2. In a small bowl, whisk the soy sauce, ½ cup of vinegar, garlic, brown sugar, peppercorns, and bay leaves.

3. If desired, in a large pan, heat the vegetable oil over medium-high heat. Place the chicken in the pan skin-side down and brown until golden, 4 to 6 minutes.

4. Place the chicken in the slow cooker, skin-side up, in one layer.

5. Pour the soy sauce mixture over the chicken, making sure the bay leaves are submerged in the liquid.

6. Cover and cook on low for 4 to 5 hours, or on high for 2 to 3 hours.

7. Season with the remaining 1 to 2 tablespoons of vinegar, as desired, at the end of cooking. Serve.

OPTION TIP: You can also cook all the ingredients in the slow cooker first, then brown the chicken afterward. Preheat the oven to broil. Transfer 1 cup of the broth and the chicken, skin-side up, to a baking dish. Broil for 2 to 3 minutes, until brown.

Per Serving: Calories: 799; Total fat: 55g; Protein: 66g; Carbs: 5g; Fiber: 0g; Sugar: 2g; Sodium: 1,712mg

MALAYSIAN CHICKEN WINGS

Prep time: 10 minutes

Cook time: 3 to 4 hours on low, 1½ to 2 hours on high, plus 5 minutes to broil

Serves 6

MALAYSIA

I love chicken wings, except when they're dry and overcooked. The slow cooker helps remedy dry wings by cooking them until tender; then, just a few minutes under a broiler to get some caramelization is all you need. These sweet and savory wings are a true favorite.

Cooking spray

3 to 3½ pounds chicken wings, split

8 garlic cloves, minced

2-inch piece fresh ginger, peeled and minced

2 tablespoons brown sugar

3 tablespoons dark soy sauce

2 tablespoons low-sodium soy sauce

½ teaspoon ground white pepper

2 tablespoons fish sauce

¼ cup honey

1 teaspoon sesame oil

1. Spray the slow cooker lightly with cooking spray.

2. In the slow cooker, arrange the chicken wings.

3. In a small bowl, whisk together the garlic, ginger, brown sugar, dark soy sauce, low-sodium soy sauce, white pepper, fish sauce, honey, and sesame oil. Pour the sauce over the chicken wings and toss gently to coat.

4. Cover and cook on low for 3 to 4 hours, or on high for 1½ to 2 hours, until the chicken is tender but not falling off the bone.

5. Preheat the oven to broil. Line a baking sheet with aluminum foil.

6. Transfer the chicken wings to the prepared baking sheet, and broil for 2 to 3 minutes, or until wings brown and char slightly. Flip and broil the other side for another 2 minutes. Serve.

OPTION TIP: If you want saucy chicken wings, at the end of cooking, transfer the sauce to a small pan and cook on the stove over medium heat until it reduces and thickens. To make it spicy, add 1 teaspoon red pepper flakes. Coat the wings with the sauce and serve. Alternatively, you can thicken the sauce in the slow cooker by adding a cornstarch-water mixture (2 tablespoons cornstarch mixed with 2 tablespoons cold water) and cooking on high for 15 minutes.

Per Serving: Calories: 631; Total fat: 41g; Protein: 49g; Carbs: 20g; Fiber: 0g; Sugar: 15g; Sodium: 1,009mg

CHINESE FIVE-SPICE WHOLE CHICKEN

CHINA

Prep time: **15 minutes**

Cook time: **5 to 6 hours on low, 3 to 4 hours on high**

Serves **6**

I was so surprised to learn that you can cook a whole chicken in a slow cooker. The result is an incredibly tender chicken—there have been times when it was so tender, it fell apart when I took it out. If you would like, you can finish the chicken in the broiler for 5 minutes to brown the skin. We love dipping the chicken in either hoisin sauce, chili sauce, or ginger-scallion sauce, accompanied by a quick vegetable side and rice.

For the chicken

1 to 2 large onions, quartered

1 (4- to 5-pound) whole chicken, giblets removed

2 tablespoons plus ½ teaspoon Chinese five-spice powder, divided

1 bulb garlic, halved

1-inch piece fresh ginger, peeled and sliced

2 tablespoons vegetable oil

¼ cup soy sauce

1 tablespoon sugar

1 teaspoon salt

To make the chicken

1. In the slow cooker, arrange enough onions so that they cover the bottom.

2. Rinse the inside and outside of the chicken. Dry the chicken with paper towels. Sprinkle ½ teaspoon of five-spice powder inside the chicken cavity, and stuff with the garlic and ginger.

3. In a small bowl, whisk together the oil, soy sauce, remaining 2 tablespoons of five-spice powder, sugar, and salt. Rub the mixture all over the chicken, getting in between the skin and meat wherever possible.

4. Place the chicken, breast-side up, in the slow cooker. For round slow cookers, place the chicken neck-side down and legs up.

5. Cover and cook on low for 5 to 6 hours, or on high for 3 to 4 hours, or until the chicken reaches 165°F. Serve with a side of rice and ginger-scallion dipping sauce, if using.

For the ginger-scallion dipping sauce (optional)

2 cups thinly sliced scallions, both white and green parts

¼ cup peeled, finely minced fresh ginger

2 teaspoons salt

⅓ cup neutral oil (vegetable or grapeseed)

To make the ginger-scallion dipping sauce, if using

In a small bowl, combine the scallions, ginger, salt, and oil, and stir together.

OPTION TIP: If desired, you can set the cooked chicken on a baking dish and broil in the oven for 5 minutes, until the skin is browned and crisp.

TECHNIQUE TIP: Some slow cookers come with a programmable thermometer probe attachment. If yours does, you can set it to automatically switch to the warm setting once your meat reaches the desired temperature.

LEFTOVERS TIP: You can make a flavorful broth in the slow cooker from the carcass and remaining chicken juices. Return the chicken carcass to the slow cooker, add water until it reaches halfway up the slow cooker, and cook on high for 4 to 5 more hours. I use this broth and leftover chicken to make a quick chicken pho noodle soup.

Per Serving: Calories: 594; Total fat: 38g; Protein: 43g; Carbs: 8g; Fiber: 1g; Sugar: 4g; Sodium: 1,149mg

THREE-CUP CHICKEN

Prep time: **15 minutes**

Cook time: **3 to 4 hours on low, 1½ to 2 hours on high**

Serves **5 or 6**

TAIWAN

This Chinese dish (*San Bei Ji*) is very popular in Taiwanese cooking. The three cups refer to a cup of sesame oil, a cup of rice wine, and a cup of soy sauce. Since there are many variations of this dish, the ratios, ingredients, and even what parts of the chicken to use are up for debate. But the end result is a flavorful and savory home-cooked meal that everyone enjoys. I like making San Bei Ji with bone-in chicken, which on the stove top usually needs to be stirred and checked on, so the slow-cooker method is a handy helper. Don't skimp on the garlic, because you really do want that much!

Cooking spray

¼ cup sesame oil

12 garlic cloves, peeled

1-inch piece fresh ginger, peeled and sliced

3 dried red chiles or 1 teaspoon red pepper flakes (optional)

3 pounds chicken drumsticks or bone-in chicken thighs

½ cup Shaoxing cooking wine or dry sherry

¼ cup light soy sauce, plus more if needed

1 tablespoon sugar

2 tablespoons cornstarch

2 tablespoons cold water

3 scallions, both white and green parts cut into 1-inch lengths

1½ cups Thai basil leaves

1. Spray the slow cooker lightly with cooking spray.

2. In a large pan, heat the sesame oil over medium heat. Add the garlic and ginger and fry until fragrant, about 1 minute. Add the red chiles or pepper flakes, if using, and fry for another 30 seconds.

3. Add the chicken to the pan and sauté for 2 to 3 minutes, flipping once, then add the cooking wine and cook for another 2 to 3 minutes to allow some of the alcohol to evaporate. Transfer the chicken to the slow cooker.

4. Add the soy sauce and sugar to the slow cooker and gently stir to combine.

5. Cover and cook on low for 3 to 4 hours, or on high for 1½ to 2 hours.

6. Transfer the chicken to a serving bowl.

7. In a small bowl, whisk together the cornstarch and cold water. Add the cornstarch mixture, scallions, and basil leaves to the slow cooker and stir. Cover and cook on high for 15 minutes, until the glaze thickens and the basil leaves have wilted.

8. Season the glaze with additional soy sauce, if needed, and pour over the chicken to coat. Serve with a side of rice.

TIME-SAVING TIP: If you're in a rush, heat up only the rice wine in a pan to release some of the alcohol. You can put everything else straight into the slow cooker.

Per Serving: Calories: 665; Total fat: 45g; Protein: 53g; Carbs: 9g; Fiber: 1g; Sugar: 3g; Sodium: 956mg

BELACAN NOT-FRIED CHICKEN

Prep time: 10 minutes

Cook time: 3 to 4 hours on low, 1½ to 2 hours on high, plus 5 minutes to broil

Serves 6 or 7

MALAYSIA

Don't get me wrong, I love fried chicken. I'll readily confess that I have a weakness for fried food, but I can't have it all the time. This alternative way of cooking belacan fried chicken satisfies my craving, and I don't live with the guilt from eating a plateful of fried food. Well, at least for that day. Belacan is a dried shrimp paste that is salty and pungent. Sometimes when I use it, I put the slow cooker outside, so don't say I didn't warn you. But once cooked, it is mighty delicious and full of salty, savory, and umami flavors.

Butter or vegetable oil,
   for greasing

2 tablespoons belacan (dried
   fermented shrimp paste)

2 tablespoons fish sauce

2 teaspoons ground coriander

1 tablespoon brown sugar

3 tablespoons vegetable oil

1 teaspoon white pepper

3 to 3½ pounds chicken
   wings, split

Juice of 1 lime

1. Grease the slow cooker with butter or oil.

2. In a large bowl, combine the belacan, fish sauce, coriander, brown sugar, oil, and white pepper. Stir to form a paste.

3. Add the chicken wings to the bowl, and rub well with the paste until they are evenly coated. Transfer the chicken to the slow cooker.

4. Cover and cook on low for 3 to 4 hours, or on high for 1½ to 2 hours, until the chicken is tender but not falling off the bone.

5. Preheat the oven to broil. Line a baking sheet with foil.

6. Transfer the chicken wings to the prepared baking sheet, and broil for 2 to 3 minutes, until the wings brown and char slightly. Flip and broil the other side for another 2 minutes.

7. Remove the wings from the oven and squeeze the lime juice over them. Serve with chili sauce.

SUBSTITUTION TIP: Belacan can be purchased at an Asian grocery store or online. But if you can't find it, you can use shrimp sauce, which is sold in most Asian grocery stores.

Per Serving: Calories: 627; Total fat: 46g; Protein: 49g; Carbs: 5g; Fiber: 0g; Sugar: 2g; Sodium: 917mg

GINGER CHICKEN

Prep time: 15 minutes
Cook time: 3 to 4 hours on low, 1½ to 2 hours on high
Serves 5 or 6

VIETNAM

This is an easy recipe for *Ga Kho Gung* that I usually prepare during the week when I have an evening meeting or school event. After my workday, I throw everything in the slow cooker, go to the meeting, and then it's done by the time I come back. The chicken is tender and savory, and highlights the flavor and aroma of ginger.

Cooking spray
3 pounds chicken drumsticks
    or bone-in thighs
2 tablespoons brown sugar
1 tablespoon chicken
    bouillon powder
1 tablespoon dark soy sauce
1 teaspoon black pepper
¼ cup fish sauce
1 cup coconut juice or water
2 tablespoons vegetable oil
2 tablespoons peeled, finely
    minced fresh ginger
1 tablespoon finely
    minced garlic
2 tablespoons cornstarch
2 tablespoons cold water
2 scallions, both white and
    green parts cut into
    2-inch lengths
Salt
1 fresh red chile, thinly sliced,
    for garnish
Fresh cilantro, for garnish
    (optional)

1. Spray the slow cooker lightly with cooking spray and add the chicken.

2. In a small bowl, whisk together the brown sugar, chicken bouillon, dark soy sauce, pepper, fish sauce, and coconut juice.

3. In a small pan, heat the oil over medium heat. Sauté the ginger and garlic until fragrant, 1 to 2 minutes, and add to the sauce. Mix well. Pour the sauce over the chicken and stir to coat.

4. Cover and cook on low for 3 to 4 hours, or on high for 1½ to 2 hours.

5. Remove the chicken from the slow cooker and arrange on a serving plate.

6. In a small bowl, mix the cornstarch and cold water. Add the cornstarch mixture and the scallions to the slow cooker.

7. Cover and cook on high for 15 minutes.

8. Season the sauce with salt. Pour the sauce over the chicken and garnish with red chile and cilantro, if using. Serve with a side of rice.

OPTION TIP: If you can get your hands on a can of coconut soda, you can use this instead of the coconut juice or water. Coconut soda is like club soda but flavored with coconut milk and will slightly sweeten the dish.

Per Serving: Calories: 506; Total fat: 27g; Protein: 51g; Carbs: 10g; Fiber: 1g; Sugar: 5g; Sodium: 1,498mg

HAINANESE CHICKEN RICE

Prep time: **10 minutes**

Cook time: **5 to 6 hours on low, 3 to 4 hours on high,** plus 30 minutes to cook rice

Serves **6**

SINGAPORE

My good friend introduced me to this dish, and I fell instantly in love. The boiled chicken was aromatic, and the rice was decadent. She made all the toppings and sauces, and I tried different variations for every bite. Although I live in an urban food mecca, there is still a dearth of restaurants here that serve this delicious dish. In fact, the next time I had it was in Asia! Hainanese Chicken Rice can be an involved process, but it's worth it. The slow cooker helps manage the time and achieves a flavorful chicken. It's up to you which toppings and side sauces you want, so have fun making your own flavor combinations.

For the chicken

1 (3- to 4-pound) whole
   chicken, giblets and
   neck removed
3 garlic cloves
1-inch piece fresh ginger,
   peeled and cut into 3 slices
3 scallions, white part only
8 cups water
1 teaspoon sesame oil

For the rice

2 tablespoons vegetable oil
5 garlic cloves, finely minced
1 tablespoon peeled finely
   minced fresh ginger
3 cups jasmine or long-
   grain rice
½ teaspoon salt, plus more
   if needed
1 English cucumber, cut
   into ¼-inch-thick slices,
   for serving
Crispy fried shallots,
   for garnish

To make the chicken

1. Rinse the inside and outside of the chicken and pat it dry with a paper towel.

2. In the slow cooker, set the chicken breast-side up, and add the garlic, ginger, scallions, and water.

3. Cover and cook on low for 5 to 6 hours, or on high for 3 to 4 hours, until the chicken reaches 165°F.

4. Transfer the chicken to a cutting board and rub the sesame oil on the chicken skin. Set aside.

To make the rice

1. Strain the broth into a large bowl or pot, then return it to the slow cooker. Cover and set on low to keep the broth warm.

2. In a large saucepan, heat the oil over medium-high heat.

3. Add the garlic and ginger and fry until fragrant, about 1 minute.

4. Add the rice and stir to coat evenly.

5. Add 4½ cups of broth from the slow cooker and the salt, and bring to a boil.

Chopped fresh cilantro,
for garnish
Kecap manis (Indonesian
sweet soy sauce),
for serving

For the ginger sauce

3 tablespoons peeled, grated
fresh ginger
2 tablespoons neutral oil
(vegetable, canola, or
grapeseed)

For the chili sauce

2 teaspoons minced garlic
2 teaspoons peeled, minced
fresh ginger
¼ cup hot sauce (like
sriracha)
½ teaspoon sugar
½ teaspoon salt
2 tablespoons freshly
squeezed lime juice

6. Cover, turn the heat down to low, and simmer until all the liquid is absorbed, about 15 minutes. Fluff with a fork when done.

7. If needed, season with additional salt. Divide among small soup bowls.

8. Carve the chicken into slices and place them on a plate with the rice and cucumber. Garnish with fried shallots and cilantro. Serve with kecap manis, ginger sauce, and chili sauce for dipping.

To make the ginger sauce

In a small bowl, mix together the ginger and oil.

To make the chili sauce

In a small bowl, mix together the garlic, ginger, hot sauce, sugar, salt, and lime juice.

TIME-SAVING TIP: You can also make the rice in a rice cooker with the chicken broth from the slow cooker. Place the garlic, ginger, and rice in the rice cooker. Follow the instructions for your rice cooker to determine how much broth to add for 3 cups uncooked rice.

Per Serving: Calories: 867; Total fat: 44g; Protein: 41g; Carbs: 76g; Fiber: 2g; Sugar: 2g; Sodium: 800mg

ROAST CHICKEN

Prep time: **15 minutes**

Cook time: **4 to 5 hours on low, 2 to 3 hours on high, plus 3 minutes to broil**

Serves **5 or 6**

One of my favorite recipes, *Ping Gai* is usually prepared with a whole chicken that is marinated, halved, laid flat, skewered, and grilled on low heat over a charcoal flame. The slow-cooker method simplifies the process without compromising on flavor, the amount of black pepper may seem like a lot, but coarsely ground peppercorn is not as spicy as finely ground pepper. Also, there's so much flavor in the sauce left over in the slow cooker that I shamelessly pour a bit on my rice. It's so good.

Cooking spray

3½ to 4 pounds bone-in, skin-on chicken thighs

1 bunch fresh cilantro (stems and leaves)

6 garlic cloves

1½ tablespoons coarsely ground black peppercorns

2 tablespoons fish sauce

2 tablespoons vegetable oil

Lime or lemon wedges, for garnish

Hot and sweet dipping sauce, for serving (optional)

1. Spray the slow cooker with cooking spray and place the chicken inside.

2. In a blender combine the cilantro, garlic, pepper, fish sauce, and oil, and process into a smooth paste. Add the paste to the slow cooker and mix to evenly coat the chicken.

3. Cover and cook on low for 4 to 5 hours, or on high for 2 to 3 hours.

4. Preheat the oven to broil. Line a baking sheet with foil.

5. Transfer the chicken to the prepared baking sheet, skin-side up, and broil for 2 to 3 minutes, until the skin is golden and charred slightly.

6. Transfer the chicken to a plate and garnish with lime or lemon wedges. Serve with hot and sweet dipping sauce (like Thai hot and sweet dipping sauce), if using, and a side of rice.

TIME-SAVING TIP: If you want to skip broiling the chicken in the oven at the end, use skinless chicken thighs.

Per Serving: Calories: 633; Total fat: 46g; Protein: 48g; Carbs: 2g; Fiber: 0g; Sugar: 0g; Sodium: 760mg

SPICY LEMONGRASS CHICKEN

VIETNAM

Prep time: 20 minutes

Cook time: 5 to 6 hours on low, 3 hours on high

Serves 5 or 6

When making *Ga Chien Sa Ot,* there's no shying away from lemongrass here, and you can control the heat from the chiles by using as few or as many as you want. The aroma and flavor of lemongrass with the heat of the chiles is a pairing made for each other. Serve this with a fresh salad or sliced cucumber.

Cooking spray

3 pounds boneless, skinless chicken thighs, cut into bite-size chunks

2 tablespoons vegetable oil

5 garlic cloves, minced

¼ cup minced lemongrass, pale green and white parts only

¼ cup minced shallots

2 to 3 Thai chiles

2 tablespoons fish sauce

2 teaspoons sugar

2 tablespoons cornstarch

2 tablespoons cold water

3 scallions, both white and green parts cut into 1-inch lengths

Salt

Fresh cilantro, for garnish

1. Spray the slow cooker with cooking spray and place the chicken inside.

2. In a small bowl, whisk together the oil, garlic, lemongrass, shallots, chiles, fish sauce, and sugar. Pour the sauce over the chicken and stir to coat.

3. Cover and cook on low for 5 to 6 hours, or on high for 3 hours.

4. In a small bowl, whisk together the cornstarch and water. Add the cornstarch mixture and the scallions to the slow cooker and stir.

5. Cover and cook on high for about 15 minutes, or until the glaze thickens.

6. Season with salt, garnish with fresh cilantro, and serve with a side of rice.

PREP IT RIGHT: Most of your prep time will be chopping up the lemongrass. You can do this up to a few days ahead and keep the minced lemongrass in the fridge until ready to use. Frozen minced lemongrass is also available at most Asian markets.

Per Serving: Calories: 394; Total fat: 17g; Protein: 54g; Carbs: 8g; Fiber: 1g; Sugar: 2g; Sodium: 829mg

STEAMED CHICKEN IN COCONUT WATER

CAMBODIA

Prep time: **15 minutes**

Cook time: **5 to 6 hours on low, 3 to 4 hours on high**

Serves **6**

This Khmer dish is very easy to make in the slow cooker. Since the chicken is steamed in coconut water, it comes out looking like, well, steamed chicken. But the aromas of lemongrass, kaffir lime leaves, and coconut water are so delicate and lovely. For a nice contrast, the chicken is accompanied by a salty and spicy chili sauce. The liquid left over after cooking is absolutely delicious, so don't waste it. Strain the broth to either pour over the chicken or ladle in a small bowl for yourself.

For the chicken

1 (4- to 5-pound) whole chicken, giblets removed

7 kaffir lime leaves, divided

4 stalks lemongrass, outer layers removed, pounded and cut into 3-inch lengths

6 (¼-inch-thick) slices peeled fresh galangal, divided

3 garlic cloves, smashed

6 scallions, both white and green parts cut into 3-inch lengths, divided

1 teaspoon salt

2 cups coconut water

1 teaspoon black peppercorns

Fresh cilantro sprigs, for garnish (optional)

1 tomato, cut into wedges, for garnish (optional)

To make the chicken

1. Rinse the inside and outside of the chicken, pat dry with a paper towel, and place it breast-side up in the slow cooker.

2. Stuff the chicken with 4 kaffir lime leaves, the lemongrass, 3 slices galangal, the garlic, and a little over half of the scallions. If you cannot fit everything in the chicken, place the rest around the chicken.

3. Rub the top of the chicken with the salt.

4. Add the coconut water, remaining 3 kaffir leaves, remaining 3 slices galangal, remaining scallions, and the peppercorns.

5. Cover and cook on low for 5 to 6 hours, or on high for 3 to 4 hours, until the chicken reaches 165°F.

6. Carve the chicken into slices. To serve, pour a ladle full of the broth on top of slices of chicken. Garnish with cilantro and/or tomato wedges, if using. Serve with the chili sauce and a side of rice.

For the chili sauce

2 to 3 red chiles, diced

2 tablespoons sugar

2 tablespoons finely
minced garlic

2 tablespoons fish sauce

¼ cup unsalted dry roasted
peanuts, chopped

1 teaspoon salt

Juice of 1 lime

To make the chili sauce

In a small bowl, whisk together the chiles, sugar, garlic, fish sauce, peanuts, salt, and lime juice.

TECHNIQUE TIP: When you salt the chicken, just sprinkle and rub the salt directly on the top. During cooking, the broth will become salty as the juices flow and the salt dissolves in it.

Per Serving: Calories: 563; Total fat: 39g; Protein: 41g; Carbs: 12g; Fiber: 2g; Sugar: 7g; Sodium: 1,478mg

KERALA THATTUKADA CHICKEN

Prep time: **15 minutes**

Cook time: **4 to 5 hours on low, 2 to 2½ hours on high,**
plus 3 minutes to broil

Serves **5 or 6**

INDIA

Kerala Thattukada Chicken is full of flavor when you combine all those tasty spices together. This dish is typically fried, but we're skipping the extra oil here by using the slow-cooker method. Having the slow cooker do the marinating and cooking for you at the same time is a bonus. Serve this dish with a side of rice, or it's nice to have with salad for a low-carb option.

Cooking spray
3 to 4 pounds chicken
    drumsticks or bone-in
    chicken thighs
5 curry leaves, finely chopped
1 tablespoon peeled, finely
    minced fresh ginger
2 tablespoons finely
    minced garlic
½ teaspoon ground turmeric
1 teaspoon ground coriander
2 teaspoons garam masala
1 teaspoon paprika
1 to 2 teaspoons ground
    cayenne pepper
1 teaspoon salt
Juice of 1 lemon
2 tablespoons vegetable oil
2 medium shallots,
    thinly sliced
3 sprigs curry leaves
1 lemon, cut into wedges,
    for garnish

1. Spray the slow cooker with cooking spray and place the chicken inside.

2. In a small bowl, mix the chopped curry leaves, ginger, garlic, turmeric, coriander, garam masala, paprika, cayenne, salt, and lemon juice until combined. Evenly coat the chicken with the mixture.

3. Cover and cook on low for 4 to 5 hours, or on high for 2 to 2½ hours.

4. Preheat the oven to broil. Line a baking sheet with foil.

5. Place the chicken on the prepared baking sheet, skin-side up, and broil for 2 to 3 minutes, until the skin is golden and charred slightly. Transfer the chicken to a serving dish.

6. In a pan, heat the oil over medium heat. Sauté the shallots and sprigs of curry leaves until soft and fragrant, 3 to 4 minutes.

7. Top the chicken with the shallots and curry leaves, and garnish with the lemon wedges.

TIME-SAVING TIP: If you want to skip broiling the chicken in the oven, use skinless chicken thighs. This dish is very flavorful so you can also save time by leaving out the sautéed shallots and curry sprigs, and dive right into the chicken.

Per Serving: Calories: 569; Total fat: 39g; Protein: 51g; Carbs: 3g; Fiber: 1g; Sugar: 0g; Sodium: 685mg

BURMESE CHILI CHICKEN

Prep time: **15 minutes**

Cook time: **4 to 5 hours on low, 2 to 2½ hours on high**

Serves **5 or 6**

MYANMAR

Burmese Chili Chicken is a spicy stir-fry that is usually cooked in a wok. But don't worry, there's no compromising on flavors when cooked in a slow cooker. The slow cooker creates a little more sauce, and there are so many layers of flavor from the spices. Serve this fiery dish with a side of rice.

Cooking spray

3 pounds boneless, skinless chicken thighs, cut into bite-size pieces

2 tablespoons vegetable oil

1 tablespoon finely minced garlic

2 teaspoons peeled, finely minced fresh ginger

1 small onion, finely diced

1 Anaheim or poblano chile, halved, seeded, and cut into ¼-inch strips

2 tablespoons fish sauce

3 teaspoons sweet paprika

2 teaspoons ground cumin

½ to 1 teaspoon ground cayenne pepper

½ teaspoon ground turmeric

2 tablespoons cornstarch

2 tablespoons cold water

1 green bell pepper, seeded and cut into ½-inch pieces

1 red bell pepper, seeded and cut into ½-inch pieces

Salt

Freshly ground black pepper

1. Spray the slow cooker with cooking spray and place the chicken inside.

2. In a medium pan, heat the oil over medium-high heat. Sauté the garlic and ginger for 1 minute, then add the onion and chile and cook until fragrant, about 2 more minutes.

3. Remove the pan from the heat and add the fish sauce, paprika, cumin, cayenne, and turmeric. Stir to combine. Add the sauce to the slow cooker, and stir to evenly coat the chicken.

4. Cover and cook on low for 4 to 5 hours, or on high for 2 to 2½ hours.

5. In a small bowl, whisk together the cornstarch and cold water. Add the cornstarch mixture, green bell pepper, and red bell pepper to the slow cooker and stir.

6. Cover and cook on high for about 15 minutes, until the glaze thickens.

7. Season with salt and ground pepper and serve.

INGREDIENT TIP: Anaheim and poblano chiles are both mild peppers that work great alongside bell peppers in dishes like this to add texture and depth. While these peppers are typically mild, the cayenne pepper gives this dish most of its heat, so be sure to add more if you like it hot or less if you prefer a milder dish.

Per Serving: Calories: 405; Total fat: 17g; Protein: 54g; Carbs: 9g; Fiber: 2g; Sugar: 2g; Sodium: 831mg

JAPAN

CHICKEN TERIYAKI

Prep time: **10 minutes**

Cook time: **4 to 5 hours on low, 2 to 2½ hours on high**

Serves **5 or 6**

Slow-cooker Chicken Teriyaki is an easy meal to make. The sauce is sweet and savory, and the dish is served with a side of rice. You will find many variations of teriyaki sauce that call for garlic or ginger, or that swap out the sake and mirin for vinegar. But here, we're going to start with the traditional standard for this delicious, quick, easy, and satisfying meal.

Cooking spray

3 pounds boneless, skinless chicken thighs, cut in bite-size chunks

½ cup sake

½ cup mirin

½ cup soy sauce

¼ cup sugar

2 tablespoons cornstarch

2 tablespoons cold water

2 teaspoons roasted sesame seeds, for garnish

1 scallion, both white and green parts thinly sliced, for garnish

1. Spray the slow cooker lightly with cooking spray and place the chicken inside.

2. In a saucepan over medium heat, combine the sake, mirin, soy sauce, and sugar and bring to a light boil for about 1 minute to allow the alcohol in the sake to evaporate. Pour the sauce over the chicken and stir to evenly coat.

3. Cover and cook on low for 4 to 5 hours, or on high for 2 to 2½ hours.

4. In a small bowl, whisk together the cornstarch and cold water. Add the cornstarch mixture to the slow cooker and stir.

5. Cover and cook on high for 15 minutes, or until the glaze thickens.

6. Garnish with the sesame seeds and scallion. Serve with a side of rice.

OPTION TIP: You can make just the teriyaki sauce on the stove top for any dish. In a saucepan, cook the sake, mirin, soy sauce, and sugar until the sauce thickens.

Per Serving: Calories: 428; Total fat: 12g; Protein: 54g; Carbs: 27g; Fiber: 1g; Sugar: 17g; Sodium: 1,887mg

LAOTIAN CHICKEN WITH MUSHROOMS

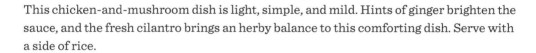

LAOS

Prep time: 30 minutes

Cook time: 4 to 5 hours on low, 2 to 2½ hours on high

Serves 5 or 6

This chicken-and-mushroom dish is light, simple, and mild. Hints of ginger brighten the sauce, and the fresh cilantro brings an herby balance to this comforting dish. Serve with a side of rice.

12 dried shiitake mushrooms
Cooking spray
3 pounds boneless, skinless chicken thighs, cut into bite-size pieces
2 tablespoons vegetable oil
2 tablespoons minced garlic
2 teaspoons peeled, grated fresh ginger
3 tablespoons fish sauce
2 teaspoons sugar
2 tablespoons cornstarch
2 tablespoons cold water
Salt
¼ cup chopped fresh cilantro

1. In a bowl, rehydrate the shiitake mushrooms with boiling water for 20 to 30 minutes. Cut off and discard the stems, and thinly slice the caps.

2. Spray the slow cooker with cooking spray and add the chicken and mushrooms.

3. In a small bowl, whisk together the oil, garlic, ginger, fish sauce, and sugar. Pour the sauce over the chicken and stir to coat.

4. Cover and cook on low for 4 to 5 hours, or on high for 2 to 2½ hours.

5. In a small bowl, whisk together the cornstarch and water. Add the cornstarch mixture to the slow cooker and stir.

6. Cover and cook on high for 15 minutes, or until the glaze thickens.

7. Season with salt and stir in the cilantro. Serve.

OPTION TIP: If you'd like more color on your chicken, you can sauté it in a pan with a little vegetable oil for a few minutes before putting it in the slow cooker.

PREP IT RIGHT: The mushrooms can be rehydrated the night before to save on prep time in the morning. Store them in an airtight container in the refrigerator until ready for use.

Per Serving: Calories: 487; Total fat: 17g; Protein: 55g; Carbs: 32g; Fiber: 4g; Sugar: 3g; Sodium: 1,110mg

KOREAN PORK WRAPS, PAGE 109

7

MEAT

BRAISED SHORT RIBS 102

CHINESE FLANK STEAK & ONIONS, AKA MONGOLIAN BEEF 103

BRAISED PORK SHOULDER 104

CAMBODIAN CARAMELIZED PORK 105

TAIWANESE BRAISED PORK BELLY BUNS 106

CHINESE-STYLE "ROASTED" LAMB 108

KOREAN PORK WRAPS 109

VIETNAMESE MEATLOAF 111

BRAISED LAMB SHANKS 113

SWEET-AND-SOUR RIBS 115

BRAISED PORK BELLY 117

BRISKET BANH MI 119

SPICY BABY BACK PORK RIBS 121

My family doesn't prepare a lot of meat during the week, but when we do, we do it with purpose. Sometimes I feel like I'm cheating when making showstopper dishes in the slow cooker, like Galbi Jjim and Braised Lamb Shanks, because it's so easy. But the slow cooker's ability to break down tough cuts of meat, coupled with a busy schedule, makes this a no-brainer for me. Oftentimes, I think to use brisket, pork shoulder, short ribs, and lamb shanks in the slow cooker, but here's a little tip: Did you know that the slow cooker can also make a delicious meatloaf? The stories are true—it comes out so moist and flavorful.

KOREA

BRAISED SHORT RIBS

Prep time: 20 minutes, plus 30 minutes to soak
Cook time: 9 to 10 hours on low, 5 to 6 hours on high
Serves 4 to 6

Growing up, we didn't eat a lot of *Galbi Jjim*. It was reserved for holidays and special occasions and, admittedly, kind of a pain in the neck to make. At least that's what my mom said. But now that I've figured out how to make it in the slow cooker, it's tempting to make on non-special-occasion days, too, thanks to its super-tender, fall-off-the-bone meat with sweet and savory soy sauce flavors. Adding a little honey at the end adds a nice gloss and a little more body to the sauce. Serve with rice and, please, find some delicious kimchi to eat with this!

Cooking spray
4 pounds beef short ribs,
    trimmed of fat
8 ounces small new
    potatoes, halved
½ cup diced Korean radish
    or daikon
1 medium onion, quartered
2 carrots, cut into
    2-inch lengths
8 garlic cloves
1-inch piece fresh ginger,
    peeled and cut into 3 slices
1 Asian pear, peeled, cored,
    and cut into large wedges
½ cup soy sauce, plus more
    if needed
¼ cup mirin
¼ cup dark brown sugar
1 teaspoon freshly ground
    black pepper
½ cup low-sodium beef stock
Honey or sugar
2 teaspoons sesame oil
¼ cup pine nuts (optional)

1. Spray the slow cooker lightly with cooking spray.

2. Rinse the ribs and, in a large bowl, soak them in cold water for 30 minutes to draw out the blood. Drain.

3. Place the ribs on the bottom of the slow cooker, then add the potatoes, radish, onion, carrots, garlic, and ginger on top.

4. In a blender combine the pear, soy sauce, mirin, brown sugar, and black pepper and process until puréed. Pour the sauce and the stock into the slow cooker.

5. Cover and cook on low for 9 to 10 hours, or on high for 5 to 6 hours.

6. Remove the ribs and vegetables from the slow cooker, and strain the cooking liquid into a bowl. Using a spoon or a fat separator, skim the fat off the liquid. Season with additional soy sauce and honey.

7. Stir the sesame oil into the cooking liquid and pour over the ribs. Garnish with pine nuts, if using, and serve.

PREP IT RIGHT: Prepare the ribs the night before. Soak, drain, and refrigerate in an airtight container until you're ready to start your meal the next day.

Per Serving: Calories: 988; Total fat: 49g; Protein: 91g; Carbs: 43g; Fiber: 6g; Sugar: 22g; Sodium: 2,270mg

CHINESE FLANK STEAK & ONIONS, AKA MONGOLIAN BEEF

CHINA

Prep time: **20 minutes**

Cook time: **3 to 4 hours on low, 1½ to 2 hours on high**

Serves **6**

This Chinese takeout favorite is so easy to make in the slow cooker. The tender, bite-size steak strips are packed with flavor from the sauce and made with less oil. Serve with a hot bowl of rice and some tender greens, and you can skip the takeout.

Cooking spray

½ cup cornstarch

2½ pounds flank steak or chuck roast, cut across the grain into ¼-inch strips

1 tablespoon vegetable oil

1 teaspoon red pepper flakes

1 large onion, thinly sliced

1-inch piece fresh ginger, peeled and julienned

5 garlic cloves, minced

½ cup low-sodium soy sauce

2 tablespoons oyster sauce

3 tablespoons Shaoxing cooking wine or dry sherry

3 tablespoons dark brown sugar

½ cup water

4 scallions, both white and green parts thinly sliced diagonally

1 teaspoon sesame oil

½ teaspoon white pepper

1. Spray the slow cooker lightly with cooking spray.

2. In a large, resealable plastic bag, add the cornstarch and beef. Seal and toss until the beef is well coated. Transfer the beef to the slow cooker.

3. In a medium pan, heat the oil over medium to medium-high heat. Add the pepper flakes, onion, ginger, and garlic, and cook until onion is slightly tender, 2 to 3 minutes. Transfer the mixture to the slow cooker.

4. In a small bowl, whisk together the soy sauce, oyster sauce, cooking wine, brown sugar, and water. Pour the sauce over the beef and mix well.

5. Cover and cook on low for 3 to 4 hours, or on high for 1½ to 2 hours.

6. Stir in the scallions, sesame oil, and white pepper. Serve with rice.

LEFTOVERS TIP: Heat up leftovers the next day and enjoy them in a hot sandwich for a filling meal.

Per Serving: Calories: 507; Total fat: 23g; Protein: 52g; Carbs: 20g; Fiber: 1g; Sugar: 7g; Sodium: 1,367mg

BRAISED PORK SHOULDER

Prep time: **20 minutes**

Cook time: **5 to 6 hours on low, 3 hours on high**

Serves **5 or 6**

INDONESIA

Kecap manis is a dark and sweet soy sauce that is used in a lot of Indonesian cuisine. Pork belly is often used for *Babi Kecap,* but I use pork shoulder here instead. The sweetness of the kecap manis comes through, and the ginger brings a delicate aroma to this rich dish. So don't skip out on grating that ginger, and watch your fingers!

Cooking spray

1 cup chicken stock

5 tablespoons kecap manis (Indonesian sweet soy sauce)

1 tablespoon dark soy sauce

Juice of 1 lemon

½ teaspoon ground black pepper

2 tablespoons vegetable oil

¾ cup shallots, thinly sliced

8 garlic cloves, minced

2 tablespoons peeled, grated fresh ginger

2½ to 3 pounds pork shoulder, cut into 1½-inch chunks

Sambal oelek, for serving

1. Spray the slow cooker lightly with cooking spray.

2. In the slow cooker, add the stock, kecap manis, dark soy sauce, lemon juice, and black pepper.

3. In a large pan, heat the oil over medium to medium-high heat. Sauté the shallots, garlic, and ginger for 3 minutes, or until fragrant, and transfer the mixture to the slow cooker.

4. Add the pork to the pan and cook for 2 to 3 minutes, until lightly browned, then transfer to the slow cooker and mix well.

5. Cover and cook on low for 5 to 6 hours, or on high for 3 hours.

6. Serve with sambal oelek and a side of rice.

INGREDIENT TIP: Sambal oelek is a hot sauce made primarily of chiles and salt. There are also some versions that use garlic, vinegar, onion, and lime or lemon juice. It's become more readily available at major grocery stores in the international foods aisle. You can also find it at Asian grocery stores or online.

Per Serving: Calories: 423; Total fat: 17g; Protein: 54g; Carbs: 11g; Fiber: 1g; Sugar: 1g; Sodium: 1,877mg

CAMBODIA

CAMBODIAN CARAMELIZED PORK

Prep time: 20 minutes

Cook time: 5 to 6 hours on low, 3 hours on high

Serves 4 or 5

Khor Sach is a flavorful pork shoulder dish with a hint of caramel flavor. The hard-boiled egg soaks up some of the flavors from the sauce and pairs well with the salty and slightly sweet pork.

Cooking spray

2 pounds pork shoulder, cut into 1½-inch chunks

2 tablespoons sugar

¼ cup plus 1 tablespoon water, divided

½ cup finely diced shallots

5 garlic cloves, minced

3 tablespoons fish sauce

1 tablespoon palm sugar, grated

1 teaspoon freshly ground black pepper

1 whole star anise

1 tablespoon soy sauce

4 or 5 hard-boiled eggs

¼ cup chopped fresh cilantro, for garnish

1. Spray the slow cooker lightly with cooking spray and place the pork inside.

2. In a small pan, heat the sugar and 1 tablespoon of water over medium-high heat until the sugar starts to bubble. Stir constantly until the sugar dissolves and begins to turn golden brown. Immediately add the remaining ¼ cup of water to the pan and stir to combine. Pour the caramel sauce into the slow cooker.

3. In the slow cooker, add the shallots, garlic, fish sauce, palm sugar, pepper, star anise, and soy sauce, and stir to combine.

4. Cover and cook on low for 5 to 6 hours, or on high for 3 hours.

5. Add the hard-boiled eggs and stir. Cover and cook on high for 15 minutes.

6. Garnish with the cilantro and serve with a side of rice.

OPTION TIP: If you want, squeeze some fresh lemon juice when the pork is plated. This is not traditional, but I like the balance between the acid from the lemon and the richness of the pork.

Per Serving: Calories: 391; Total fat: 15g; Protein: 51g; Carbs: 12g; Fiber: 0g; Sugar: 7g; Sodium: 1,948mg

TAIWANESE BRAISED PORK BELLY BUNS

Prep time: **15 minutes**

Cook time: **6 to 7 hours on low, 4 hours on high**

Serves **6**

TAIWAN

Okay, so we're not making the steamed buns in the slow cooker here. You can purchase fresh or frozen buns from an Asian market. It's the pork belly that shines in *Gua Boa* and comes out oh-so delicious from the slow cooker. The little strips of pork belly are packed with flavor, so you need only a couple of slices in each bun. This is a popular snack food in Taiwan and is usually eaten with some chopped pickled mustard greens. But even without the greens, these are still a crowd pleaser.

Cooking spray

2 tablespoons vegetable oil

2 pounds pork belly, skin on, cut lengthwise into 2-inch strips, then crosswise into ¼-inch slices

6 garlic cloves, crushed

¾-inch piece fresh ginger, peeled and thinly sliced

2 whole star anise

3 tablespoons brown sugar, divided

1 teaspoon five-spice powder

1 teaspoon white pepper

⅓ cup light soy sauce

2 tablespoons dark soy sauce

¼ cup Shaoxing cooking wine or dry sherry

¼ cup water

¾ cup roasted unsalted peanuts

1. Spray the slow cooker lightly with cooking spray.

2. In large pan, heat the oil over medium-high heat. Add the pork belly and cook until lightly browned, about 2 minutes on each side. Transfer to the slow cooker.

3. In a small bowl, mix together the garlic, ginger, star anise, 2 tablespoons of brown sugar, five-spice powder, white pepper, light and dark soy sauces, and cooking wine. Pour the sauce and water over the pork and mix to incorporate.

4. Cover and cook on low for 6 to 7 hours, or on high for 4 hours.

5. In a food processor or blender, combine the peanuts and the remaining 1 tablespoon of brown sugar and process until coarsely ground. Alternatively, you can place the peanuts in a resealable plastic bag and gently crush with a rolling pin, then mix with the brown sugar. Set aside.

12 to 15 Chinese-style
steamed white buns, fresh
or frozen

½ cup chopped Asian pickled
mustard greens (optional)

¼ cup chopped fresh cilantro,
for garnish

6. Prepare the white buns according to package instructions.

7. To serve, place 1 or 2 slices pork belly and some pickled mustard greens, if using, in each steamed bun. Sprinkle with the sugared peanuts and garnish with the cilantro.

INGREDIENT TIP: Pickled mustard greens can be found in most Asian grocery stores. If you cannot find them, you can omit this ingredient.

OPTION TIP: You can add a little hoisin sauce to the bun, or add a little sauce that is left over from the slow cooker.

Per Serving: Calories: 1,059; Total fat: 95g; Protein: 24g; Carbs: 26g; Fiber: 3g; Sugar: 5g; Sodium: 1,351mg

CHINA

CHINESE-STYLE "ROASTED" LAMB

Prep time: **20 minutes**

Cook time: **4 to 5 hours on low, 2 to 3 hours on high**

Serves **5 or 6**

Lamb shoulder, forequarter, shank, and neck are preferred cuts for the slow cooker, and this recipe for *Char Siu Lamb* uses boneless lamb shoulder. Char Siu is a roasted dish that is typically made with pork, but this spin on a classic is for the folks who love lamb. Cooking it on low heat is preferred since we're skipping the marinating time here, and the meat comes out tender.

Cooking spray
1 tablespoon vegetable oil
3 pounds boneless lamb
    shoulder, cut into long
    3-inch-thick strips
3 garlic cloves, minced
¼ cup hoisin sauce
1 tablespoon sugar
2 tablespoons soy sauce
2 tablespoons Shaoxing
    cooking wine or dry sherry
3 tablespoons honey, divided
1 teaspoon five-spice powder
½ teaspoon sesame oil
¼ cup water

1. Spray the slow cooker lightly with cooking spray.

2. In a large pan, heat the oil over medium-high heat. Cook the lamb until browned on all sides, about 5 minutes. Transfer to the slow cooker.

3. In a small bowl, whisk the garlic, hoisin, sugar, soy sauce, cooking wine, 2 tablespoons of honey, five-spice powder, sesame oil, and water. Pour the sauce over the lamb and evenly coat.

4. Cover and cook on low for 4 to 5 hours, or on high for 2 to 3 hours.

5. Transfer the lamb to a cutting board and brush with the remaining 1 tablespoon of honey.

6. Carve the lamb into ½-inch slices and arrange on a serving plate. Spoon the sauce over the lamb slices and serve with a side of rice.

LEFTOVERS TIP: Chop up leftover Char Sui Lamb and make fried rice.

Per Serving: Calories: 420; Total fat: 16g; Protein: 47g; Carbs: 20g; Fiber: 1g; Sugar: 15g; Sodium: 712mg

KOREAN PORK WRAPS

Prep time: 20 minutes

Cook time: 6 to 7 hours on low, 4 hours on high

Serves 6

KOREA

Whenever I think of coming together and sharing food, I think of *Bo Ssam*. It is served family style with all the food in the middle of the table. Everyone creates their own custom bundles of pork and toppings all wrapped in a leaf of lettuce or salted cabbage. You can add rice to your wrap if you choose, but I often omit it and stuff my wraps with pork and lots of toppings which can be extensive, from sliced garlic and fresh chiles to perilla leaves, spicy radish salad, and even fresh oysters! But you can simplify your fillings to just pork and *ssamjang* sauce, since the pork is so delicious and tender on its own. We cook the pork with brewed coffee and stout to add deeper flavors and minimize some of the gamy smell, and I prefer to use my slow cooker for this dish.

For the pork

1 to 2 yellow onions, quartered

½ cup stout or porter beer

½ cup brewed coffee

3 pounds pork belly or pork shoulder

3 tablespoons peeled, minced fresh ginger

4 tablespoons minced garlic

2 tablespoons doenjang (Korean fermented soybean paste)

1 tablespoon brown sugar or honey

½ teaspoon ground black pepper

2 bunches red leaf lettuce, for wraps

To make the pork

1. Place enough onions in the slow cooker to cover the bottom. Add the stout and coffee.

2. Place the pork on top of the onions.

3. In a small bowl, combine the ginger, garlic, doenjang, brown sugar, and pepper into a paste, and evenly coat the pork.

4. Cover and cook on low for 6 to 7 hours, or on high for 4 hours.

5. Transfer the pork to a cutting board and cut it into ¼-inch-thick slices.

6. Serve with the lettuce leaves, sauce, toppings, and rice.

> **CONTINUED**

Korean Pork Wraps

> **CONTINUED**

For the sauce

¼ cup doenjang (Korean
    fermented soybean paste)
2 tablespoons gochujang
    (Korean red chili paste)
1 tablespoon sesame oil
1 teaspoon minced garlic
2 tablespoons minced onion
2 tablespoons thinly
    sliced scallion
1 tablespoon roasted
    sesame seeds
2 teaspoons sugar or honey
    (optional)

Optional toppings

Spicy Radish Salad
    (page 148)
Perilla or shiso leaves
Fresh oysters
Fresh chiles, sliced
Garlic cloves, sliced

To make the sauce

In a small bowl, mix the doenjang, gochujang, sesame oil, garlic, onion, scallion, sesame seeds, and sugar, if using.

OPTION TIP: After the pork is done in the slow cooker, you can crisp up the skin in a pan over medium heat, or put it on a baking sheet under the broiler for about 3 minutes.

TIME-SAVING TIP: Ssamjang can be bought premade at Korean grocery stores, and you can even find it online.

Per Serving: Calories: 368; Total fat: 14g; Protein: 45g; Carbs: 12g; Fiber: 2g; Sugar: 4g; Sodium: 1,288mg

VIETNAMESE MEATLOAF

Prep time: 20 minutes

Cook time: 4 to 5 hours on low, 2 to 3 hours on high

Serves 4 or 5

VIETNAM

Cha Trung is a steamed meat-and-egg meatloaf with great flavor and texture from the noodles and mushrooms. I have found that it turns out great in a slow cooker. The low-and-slow method coupled with the fact that the slow cooker traps moisture prevents the meatloaf from getting dry. For extra punch, serve it with *nuoc cham* (Vietnamese dipping sauce).

For the meatloaf

Cooking spray

2 ounces dried mung bean thread vermicelli

1 pound ground pork

8 ounces ground beef

¼ cup thinly sliced wood ear mushrooms

¼ cup finely diced shallots

3 large eggs, lightly beaten

1 tablespoon fish sauce

¼ teaspoon salt

½ teaspoon black pepper

2 egg yolks

2 scallions, both white and green parts thinly sliced, for garnish

Cucumber slices, for serving

To make the meatloaf

1. Line the slow cooker with aluminum foil, and spray the foil with cooking spray.

2. In a bowl, cover the bean thread vermicelli in hot water and soak for 15 minutes.

3. While the noodles are soaking, in a large bowl, combine the pork, beef, mushrooms, shallots, eggs, fish sauce, salt, and black pepper.

4. Drain the bean thread vermicelli and roughly chop it into ½-inch lengths. Add to the bowl and stir to combine.

5. Transfer the mixture to the slow cooker, and pack it firmly into a loaf.

6. Cover and cook on low for 4 to 5 hours, or on high for 2 to 3 hours.

7. In a small bowl, whisk the egg yolks and lightly brush them over the loaf.

8. Cover and cook on high for 15 minutes, or until egg yolks are cooked. Using the foil lining, lift the meatloaf out of the slow cooker.

9. Garnish with the scallions. Serve with cucumber slices and nuoc cham, if using, and a side of rice.

> **CONTINUED**

Vietnamese Meatloaf

> **CONTINUED**

For the nuoc cham (optional)

2 fresh red chiles (like Thai red chiles), thinly sliced

1 garlic clove, finely minced

¼ cup freshly squeezed lime juice

3 tablespoons sugar

3 tablespoons fish sauce

¼ cup warm water

To make the nuoc cham, if using

In a small bowl, combine the chiles, garlic, lime juice, sugar, fish sauce, and warm water. Mix well.

OPTION TIP: You can double the recipe for 6-quart or larger slow cookers.

Per Serving: Calories: 519; Total fat: 36g; Protein: 36g; Carbs: 7g; Fiber: 0g; Sugar: 1g; Sodium: 671mg

BRAISED LAMB SHANKS

Prep time: 20 minutes

Cook time: 6 to 7 hours on low, 5 to 6 hours on high

Serves 4 to 6

INDIA

In my opinion, low and slow is the best way to cook lamb shanks. Not only do these lamb shanks taste amazing with all the incredible spices and the tenderness of the meat, but it looks like you spent all day cooking. So, take care and brown the meat, fry up the spices, and sauté those onions before throwing it all in the slow cooker. Let the slow cooker do what it does best and handle the rest.

Cooking spray

2 tablespoons vegetable oil,
plus more if needed

4 to 6 lamb shanks

1 cinnamon stick

5 cardamom pods

5 whole cloves

2 medium onions, thinly sliced

2 tablespoons minced garlic

2 teaspoons peeled, minced
fresh ginger

3 tomatoes, chopped

2 teaspoons Kashmiri
chili powder

1 tablespoon ground
coriander

2 teaspoons ground cumin

1 teaspoon ground turmeric

1 teaspoon salt, plus more
if needed

1 cup water

4 tablespoons plain whole
milk or reduced-fat yogurt

½ tablespoons garam masala

¼ cup chopped fresh cilantro,
for garnish

1. Spray the slow cooker with cooking spray.

2. In a large pan, heat the oil over medium-high heat. Working in batches, brown the lamb shanks on all sides, about 3 minutes on each side. Transfer the lamb to the slow cooker.

3. If needed, add up to 2 more tablespoons of vegetable oil to the pan and heat over medium heat. Add the cinnamon stick, cardamom pods, and cloves, and fry for 1 minute.

4. Add the onions, garlic, and ginger, and sauté until the onions turn light brown, about 5 minutes.

5. Remove the pan from the heat and add the tomatoes, Kashmiri chili powder, coriander, cumin, turmeric, and salt. Mix well.

6. Pour the sauce into the slow cooker and evenly coat the lamb shanks. Add the water.

> **CONTINUED**

Braised Lamb Shanks

> CONTINUED

7. Cover and cook on low for 6 to 7 hours, or on high for 5 to 6 hours, until the lamb is tender.

8. Transfer the lamb shanks to a serving platter. Discard the cinnamon stick.

9. In the slow cooker, whisk in the yogurt and garam masala, and season with salt. Pour the sauce over the lamb shanks and garnish with the cilantro. Serve with naan, rice, or salad.

SUBSTITUTION TIP: If you cannot find Kashmiri chili powder, use 1½ teaspoon paprika plus ½ teaspoon cayenne pepper.

TIME-SAVING TIP: If you are short on time, skip the browning process and put the shanks right in the slow cooker, then proceed with step 3.

Per Serving: Calories: 524; Total fat: 27g; Protein: 36g; Carbs: 32g; Fiber: 7g; Sugar: 12g; Sodium: 1,836mg

SWEET-AND-SOUR RIBS

Prep time: **20 minutes**

Cook time: **7 to 8 hours on low, 4 hours on high**

Serves **4 to 6**

CHINA

Tang Cu Xiao Pai is incredibly succulent, and cooking them at a low temperature is highly recommended. Chinese black vinegar is the sour element used here for the sweet-and-sour sauce. Most Western versions add a tomato-based element, like ketchup or tomato paste. I've used a little bit of that influence and added some tomato paste here, although it's not necessary. It's a bit of a process making these ribs the traditional way, but they're so easy to make in the slow cooker.

Cooking spray

¼ cup white flour

¼ cup brown sugar

2 tablespoons Shaoxing cooking wine or dry sherry

2 tablespoons soy sauce

¼ cup Chinese black vinegar

2 teaspoons peeled, grated fresh ginger

2 tablespoons tomato paste (optional)

⅓ cup water

1 onion, cut into thick wedges

3 pounds pork spareribs, cut into 2- to 3-rib sections

1. Spray the slow cooker with cooking spray, or for easier cleanup, line the slow cooker with aluminum foil and spray the foil with cooking spray.

2. In a saucepan, combine the flour, brown sugar, cooking wine, soy sauce, black vinegar, ginger, tomato paste (if using), and water. Whisk constantly over medium heat until the sauce thickens, 5 to 10 minutes.

3. Turn the heat off and set the sauce aside. Reserve ½ cup of sauce and store in the refrigerator for later.

4. Place a layer of ribs in the slow cooker, coat with half of the sauce from the pan, and add half the onion. Repeat with the remaining ribs, sauce, and onion. Cover and cook on low for 7 to 8 hours, or on high for 4 hours.

> **CONTINUED**

Sweet-and-Sour Ribs

> **CONTINUED**

5. Preheat the oven to broil. Line a baking sheet with foil.

6. Transfer the ribs to the prepared baking sheet and brush them with the sauce from slow cooker. Broil the ribs for 2 to 3 minutes, or until they brown and char slightly.

7. In a small saucepan, reheat the reserved sauce, brush it on the ribs, and serve.

SUBSTITUTION TIP: If you cannot find Chinese black vinegar, you can use balsamic vinegar instead. Balsamic vinegar is a little sweeter, so you might want to cut the amount of brown sugar by about a tablespoon.

TIME-SAVING TIP: You can serve the ribs without finishing them in the oven. Just brush them with the reserved sauce and dig in.

Per Serving: Calories: 751; Total fat: 38g; Protein: 71g; Carbs: 19g; Fiber: 1g; Sugar: 10g; Sodium: 646mg

BRAISED PORK BELLY

Prep time: 20 minutes

Cook time: 5 to 6 hours on low, 3 to 4 hours on high

Serves 5 or 6

JAPAN

I think pork belly was meant to be cooked low and slow as it needs time to render the fat and melt the collagen. There is a preliminary cooking process for *Kakuni* to help reduce fat and minimize some of the gamy pork smell before the pork belly is simmered in the sauce in the slow cooker. We like making *donburi* bowls with a few slices of pork, egg, and blanched spinach on top of rice, and use *karashi*, a Japanese hot mustard, for dipping.

Cooking spray

2 pounds pork belly, skin on, cut lengthwise into 2-inch strips

2-inch piece fresh ginger, peeled and thinly sliced

2 scallions, both white and green parts cut into 2-inch lengths

2 cups dashi stock (1 teaspoon dashi powder dissolved in 2 cups hot water)

½ cup sake

⅓ cup mirin

¼ cup sugar

½ cup soy sauce

4 hard-boiled eggs, peeled (optional)

Karashi (Japanese hot mustard), for serving (optional)

1. Spray the slow cooker lightly with cooking spray.

2. In a stockpot, place the pork belly, ginger, and scallions. Fill the pot with water until it covers the meat. Boil for 10 to 15 minutes.

3. While the pork is cooking, in the slow cooker combine the stock, sake, mirin, sugar, and soy sauce.

4. Remove the pork from the pot and gently rinse with cold water. Discard the water, scallions, and ginger.

5. Cut the pork into 2-inch slices and transfer to the slow cooker.

6. Cover and cook on low for 5 to 6 hours, or on high for 3 to 4 hours.

7. Add the hard-boiled eggs, if using, to the slow cooker.

8. Cover and cook on high for 15 minutes.

> **CONTINUED**

Braised Pork Belly

> **CONTINUED**

9. Using a slotted spoon, remove the pork and eggs and place them on a plate lined with paper towels.

10. Using a spoon or fat separator, remove the fat from the sauce.

11. Cut the pork slices and eggs in half and place over bowls of rice (if making rice bowls) or in a serving dish.

12. Drizzle a little sauce over the pork. Serve with karashi, if using, for dipping.

INGREDIENT TIP: Karashi can be purchased at most Asian grocery stores.

Per Serving: Calories: 1,036; Total fat: 96g; Protein: 17g; Carbs: 21g; Fiber: 0g; Sugar: 15g; Sodium: 1,635mg

BRISKET BANH MI

Prep time: 20 minutes, plus 1 hour to prepare pickles
Cook time: 8 to 9 hours on low, 4 to 5 hours on high
Serves 6 or 7

VIETNAM

There are definitely certain kinds of meat that cook well in slow cookers (chicken thighs, pork shoulder, beef chuck, and lamb shanks, to name a few), and brisket is on my list. This isn't a traditional recipe, but I'm using flavors from Vietnam to create banh mi sandwiches. *Banh mi* refers to bread, particularly, a French baguette. It is usually packed with meat, cucumber slices, pickled radish and carrots (*do chua*), sliced jalapeños, cilantro, and pâté. The great thing about brisket is that if you have any left over, it's even better the next day.

For the do chua

2 medium carrots, cut into
    matchsticks
1 small daikon, cut into
    matchsticks
1 teaspoon salt
2 tablespoons plus
    2 teaspoons sugar, divided
⅓ cup warm water
½ cup white vinegar

To make the do chua

1. In a large bowl, mix together the carrots, daikon, salt, and 2 teaspoons of sugar. Knead gently until liquid comes out of the vegetables. Set aside for 15 minutes.

2. Meanwhile, in a small bowl, stir the warm water, vinegar, and remaining 2 tablespoons of sugar until dissolved.

3. Rinse the carrots and daikon in a colander and drain. Gently squeeze the water from the vegetables and place them in one large or two small mason jars.

4. Pour the vinegar mixture into the jar until the vegetables are submerged.

5. Cover and set aside in the refrigerator for at least 1 hour or until ready to use.

> **CONTINUED**

Brisket Banh Mi

> CONTINUED

For the banh mi

Cooking spray

1 large onion, thinly sliced

2 cups low-sodium beef broth

1 (2½-pound) beef brisket

1 teaspoon salt

¼ cup brown sugar

¼ cup shallots, finely minced

⅓ cup finely minced
    lemongrass, pale green and
    white parts only

2 tablespoons minced garlic

2 tablespoons fish sauce

1 tablespoon soy sauce

2 tablespoons vegetable oil

1 teaspoon freshly ground
    black pepper

1 teaspoon ground cumin

1 cinnamon stick

2 whole star anise

4 whole cloves

Juice of 1 lime

4 to 6 (8-inch) baguette rolls,
    halved lengthwise

Mayonnaise

1 cucumber, sliced

5 jalapeños, thinly sliced

½ bunch fresh
    cilantro, chopped

To make the banh mi

1. Spray the slow cooker with cooking spray.

2. Arrange the onion on the bottom of the slow cooker and pour in the broth. Place the brisket on top of the onion, fat-side up, and season with the salt.

3. In a small bowl or blender, mix the brown sugar, shallots, lemongrass, garlic, fish sauce, soy sauce, oil, pepper, and cumin into a paste.

4. Spread the paste on top of the brisket, and add the cinnamon stick, star anise, and cloves to the broth.

5. Cover and cook on low for 8 to 9 hours, or on high for 4 to 5 hours.

6. Transfer the brisket to a cutting board and cut against the grain into thin slices or shred using a fork. Squeeze the lime juice over the brisket.

7. Assemble the sandwiches by spreading the bread with mayonnaise, then adding a few pieces of brisket, cucumber and jalapeño slices, cilantro, and do chua.

TIME-SAVING TIP: The do chua can be made in advance and stored in the refrigerator for up to 2 weeks.

PREP IT RIGHT: Speed up your prep time by making the spice paste for the banh mi in step 3 the night before and storing it in an airtight container in the refrigerator until ready for use.

Per Serving: Calories: 504; Total fat: 18g; Protein: 46g; Carbs: 41g; Fiber: 3g; Sugar: 15g; Sodium: 1,793mg

SPICY BABY BACK PORK RIBS

KOREA

Prep time: **15 minutes**

Cook time: **4 to 5 hours on low, 2 to 3 hours on high,**
plus 3 minutes to broil

Serves **7 or 8**

Daeji Galbi is one of my favorite barbecue dishes, but I often forget to plan for the marinating time. Luckily, the slow cooker helps this process along, and you can start cooking the ribs without marinating them first. The star ingredient here is gochujang, a fermented red chili paste. With a quick broil in the oven at the end, you've got yourself some tasty ribs that are sure to be a crowd favorite.

Cooking spray
½ onion
8 garlic cloves
2 (1-inch-long) thin slices peeled fresh ginger
¼ cup soy sauce
1 cup gochujang (Korean red chili paste)
¼ cup mirin
2 tablespoons granulated sugar
2 tablespoons dark brown sugar
2 teaspoons freshly ground black pepper
1 tablespoon sesame oil
2 racks baby back ribs, about 5 pounds

1. Spray the slow cooker with cooking spray, or for easier cleanup, line the slow cooker with aluminum foil and spray the foil with cooking spray.

2. In a blender process the onion, garlic, ginger, soy sauce, gochujang, mirin, granulated sugar, brown sugar, pepper, and sesame oil until smooth.

3. Cut the ribs into individual rib sections.

4. In the slow cooker, add the ribs and marinade, making sure the ribs are all coated well.

5. Cover and cook on low for 4 to 5 hours, or on high for 2 to 3 hours.

6. Preheat the oven to broil. Line a baking sheet with foil.

7. Transfer the ribs to the prepared baking sheet, and spoon the sauce from the slow cooker over them.

8. Broil for 2 to 3 minutes, or until ribs brown and char slightly.

OPTION TIP: If you have time and want to marinate the ribs first, place the ribs and marinade in a resealable plastic bag. Seal and marinate in the refrigerator for at least 4 hours, or as long as overnight.

Per Serving: Calories: 1,103; Total fat: 85g; Protein: 55g; Carbs: 30g; Fiber: 1g; Sugar: 18g; Sodium: 1,244mg

INDONESIAN STEAMED COCONUT CUPCAKE, PAGE 131

8

DESSERT

MATCHA & COCONUT MOCHI CAKE 124

BLACK STICKY RICE PUDDING 126

SWEET RICE PUNCH 127

BLACK SESAME CHEESECAKE 129

INDONESIAN STEAMED COCONUT CUPCAKE 131

COCONUT CUSTARD 133

ASIAN PEAR UPSIDE-DOWN CAKE 135

MANGO COMPOTE 137

When I was growing up, my mom didn't make a lot of desserts. Dessert was basically cut-up fresh fruit at the end of a meal. Although this was a healthier route, I think it made me become obsessed with all kinds of desserts. For desserts that are either steamed or baked in a water bath, the slow cooker handles them with ease. It also gives great results, producing moist cakes, creamy custards, and velvety cheesecakes.

JAPAN

MATCHA & COCONUT MOCHI CAKE

Prep time: **20 minutes**

Cook time: **2½ to 3 hours on high**

Makes **9 large pieces or 16 small pieces**

Mochi is a chewy rice cake that is traditionally made by pounding glutinous rice with a large wooden mallet while another person turns the rice and adds water. Lucky for us, we can make our own mochi out of *mochiko* (sweet rice flour). Don't expect a crumbly cake. This is a dense and bouncy cake that is so easy to make. And making this cake in a slow cooker brings out more matcha flavor and results in a chewier texture. I admit that there are many times when I've nibbled on a few squares in the car while running errands. If you'd like, sprinkle some powdered sugar on top!

Cooking spray or butter,
   for greasing

4 tablespoons butter, melted
   and slightly cooled

2 large eggs

¾ cup evaporated milk

¾ cup coconut milk

1½ cups mochiko (glutinous
   sweet rice flour)

¾ cup sugar

3 teaspoons matcha powder

1 teaspoon baking powder

Powdered sugar (optional)

1. Set a rack inside your slow cooker. If do not have a rack, make an aluminum foil coil that is 1½ inches thick in diameter. Wrap the slow cooker lid tightly with a kitchen towel, tying the ends up on top, to prevent condensation on the lid from dripping on to the cake.

2. Lightly spray with cooking spray or butter the sides of 6-inch round baking pan, and line the bottom with parchment paper. If you have an oval slow cooker, you can use a 9-by-5-inch loaf pan. Set aside.

3. In a large bowl, beat the melted butter and eggs together until smooth. Add the evaporated milk and coconut milk, and mix until combined.

4. In a separate bowl, whisk together the rice flour, sugar, matcha, and baking powder. Add the dry mixture to the wet mixture, and whisk to blend.

5. Pour the batter into the prepared baking dish until it is three-quarters full, then place the dish inside the slow cooker.

6. Cover and cook on high for 2½ to 3 hours, or until a toothpick inserted in the middle comes out clean.

7. Slightly cool on a baking rack before transferring the cake to a cutting board.

8. Sprinkle powdered sugar, if using, on top before cutting into squares.

OPTION TIP: For those who do not like the taste of matcha, you can omit it and still have a delicious mochi cake.

TECHNIQUE TIP: Sometimes the mochi cake will rise and then fall quickly once some air releases from the sides of the pan, so don't fret if this happens to your cake!

LEFTOVERS TIP: Refrigerate your cake after a day in an airtight container. After that, you can freeze it.

Per Serving (large piece): Calories: 296; Total fat: 13g; Protein: 5g; Carbs: 41g; Fiber: 1g; Sugar: 20g; Sodium: 78mg

BLACK STICKY RICE PUDDING

Prep time: **5 minutes**

Cook time: **8 hours on low**

Serves **4 to 6**

I like cooking *Kao Niew Dum* in the slow cooker because I don't have to worry about soaking the rice overnight. This dessert is a thick rice pudding made of unhulled glutinous rice that is not actually black but instead a deep, dark purple. The rice is sweet and topped with rich coconut milk. You can add a pinch of salt to your coconut milk so that there is a slight contrast of sweet and savory flavors. We often eat this with sliced mango or strawberries.

Cooking spray

1 cup black glutinous rice

¼ teaspoon salt

1 pandan leaf, knotted
    (optional)

3¼ cups water

⅓ cup finely chopped palm
    sugar, plus more to
    taste (or 3 tablespoons
    brown sugar)

½ cup coconut milk

Grated coconut, for garnish
    (optional)

Roasted sesame seeds, for
    garnish (optional)

1. Spray a 4- to 5-quart slow cooker lightly with cooking spray. If using a larger slow cooker, you will need to double the recipe.

2. In the slow cooker, add the rice, salt, pandan leaf (if using), and water.

3. Cover and cook on low for 8 hours.

4. Remove the pandan leaf and stir in the palm sugar until melted. Add more sugar to taste, if desired.

5. Serve warm in small bowls with a spoonful or two of coconut milk on top. Garnish with grated coconut and/ or sesame seeds, if using.

INGREDIENT TIP: Pandan leaves are used as a flavoring in various Southeast Asian cuisines. They are fragrant and have a vanilla-like essence.

OPTION TIP: If you prefer, you can also chill the rice pudding in the refrigerator for 1 to 2 hours and serve cold.

DIET TIP: You can use light coconut milk for serving if you want to reduce the fat content.

Per Serving: Calories: 309; Total fat: 8g; Protein: 4g; Carbs: 56g; Fiber: 2g; Sugar: 15g; Sodium: 209mg

SWEET RICE PUNCH

Prep time: **10 minutes, plus 1 to 3 hours to soak**

Cook time: **4 to 6 hours on low**

Serves **7 to 8**

KOREA

When I was little, my grandmother made *Shikhye* for us every summer. I remember the malted barley flour (*yeotgireum-garu*) soaking overnight, and then it was on the stove most of the next day. When I found out what the process was as an adult, I felt a little guilty that we kids went through batches of Shikhye so quickly! This refreshing punch is believed to aid digestion, which is why it is served after a meal. It has to be cooked at a constant warm temperature of about 140°F for many hours to allow for the rice to lightly ferment in a malt barley liquid, which is why the slow cooker is a perfect vessel for making this punch. When I told my mom that you can use the warm function on the slow cooker to make Shikhye, she responded with wide eyes, "정말?" ("Really?") Totally, Mom. You can.

1¼ cups yeotgireum-garu
(malted barley flour)

12 cups warm water

2 cups cooked short-grain
rice, chilled or room
temperature

¾ cup sugar, divided, plus
more if needed

1 cinnamon stick (optional)

Pine nuts, for garnish
(optional)

Dried jujubes, thinly sliced,
for garnish (optional)

1. In a large bowl or stockpot, stir together the malted barley flour and warm water. Let the flour soak undisturbed for 1 to 3 hours. The longer it soaks, the better the flavor.

2. In the slow cooker, place the cooked rice and 6 tablespoons of sugar.

3. Once the flour has soaked, gently pour the liquid into the slow cooker, leaving the barley sediment behind in the bowl. Discard the sediment.

4. Cover and set on the warm function for 4 to 6 hours, until a few grains of rice start to float to the top. This means the rice has fermented.

5. Strain the shikhye through a fine-mesh strainer lined with cheesecloth into a large stockpot, reserving the rice.

> **CONTINUED**

Sweet Rice Punch

> CONTINUED

6. Add the remaining 6 tablespoons of sugar and the cinnamon stick, if using, to the stockpot, and boil the liquid for about 10 minutes. Lower the heat and skim off any foam. Taste for sweetness and add more sugar if needed.

7. Turn off the heat. Once the liquid has cooled slightly, place it in the refrigerator until cold, 3 to 4 hours.

8. Rinse the reserved rice under cold water, drain, and store in a container in the refrigerator.

9. When ready to serve, ladle punch into cups or small bowls, add a spoonful of rice to each, and garnish with pine nuts and/or jujubes, if using.

INGREDIENT TIP: Yeotgireum-garu is barley flour that has undergone the malting process, converting the starches into maltose. Make sure that you do not use malted milk powder, as people can confuse the two. You can purchase yeotgireum-garu online or in a Korean grocery store. Bob's Red Mill brand also produces a malted barley flour.

Per Serving: Calories: 379; Total fat: 1g; Protein: 8g; Carbs: 87g; Fiber: 5g; Sugar: 22g; Sodium: 7mg

BLACK SESAME CHEESECAKE

Prep time: 20 minutes

Cook time: 1½ to 2 hours on high

Serves 6

JAPAN

Years ago, I started gobbling up ice cream sandwiches made with black sesame ice cream. Black sesame seeds have a nutty flavor that is slightly bitter, and they are pretty amazing when paired with something sweet, like ice cream or cheesecake. Slow cookers cook cheesecake with the right amount of heat and moisture, achieving a smooth and uncracked surface. You have the option to go the extra mile and add a salted caramel sauce to your cheesecake. I highly recommend it!

For the cheesecake

Cooking spray

1 cup graham cracker crumbs

3 tablespoons unsalted butter, melted

½ cup plus 1 tablespoon sugar, divided

¾ cup roasted black sesame seeds

16 ounces cream cheese, at room temperature

2 tablespoons all-purpose flour

1 teaspoon vanilla extract

2 large eggs

½ cup sour cream

To make the cheesecake

1. Place a rack or an aluminum foil coil that is about 2 inches thick in the slow cooker. Pour hot water to the top of the rack or coil. Wrap the slow cooker lid tightly with a kitchen towel, tying the ends up on top, to prevent condensation on the lid from dripping on to the cake.

2. Spray a 6-inch springform pan with cooking spray and line the bottom with parchment paper. Set aside.

3. In medium bowl, combine the graham cracker crumbs, butter, and 1 tablespoon of sugar. Press the crumb mixture evenly on the bottom of the pan and about 1 inch up on the sides.

4. In a food processor, pulse the sesame seeds until they resemble a coarse powder. Transfer to a bowl and set aside. Remove the food processor blade, wipe the inside of the food processor and the blade, and return the blade to the bowl.

5. In the food processor bowl, combine the cream cheese, remaining ½ cup of sugar, flour, and vanilla, and process until smooth. Scrape down the sides of the bowl.

6. Add the eggs to the cream cheese mixture and process until combined. Add the sour cream and sesame seeds, and process until smooth.

> **CONTINUED**

Black Sesame Cheesecake

> **CONTINUED**

For the salted caramel sauce (optional)

¾ cup brown sugar
⅓ cup unsalted butter
3 tablespoons half-and-half
½ teaspoon salt, or more to taste
1 teaspoon vanilla extract

7. Pour the batter into the prepared springform pan, and gently tap the pan to release air bubbles.

8. Place the pan in the slow cooker.

9. Cover and cook on high for 1½ to 2 hours, until the cake center registers 155°F.

10. With the lid on, turn the slow cooker off and let the cake rest inside for 1 hour to cool.

11. Remove the lid, transfer the pan to a cooling rack, and run a warm paring knife along the sides of the cheesecake. Cool to room temperature.

12. Chill the cheesecake in the refrigerator for at least 4 hours or overnight.

13. Release and remove the outer ring of the pan, and place the cheesecake on a plate.

14. Slice with a warm, dry knife, and serve with caramel sauce, if using, and/or whipped cream.

To make the salted caramel sauce, if using

1. In a small saucepan over medium-low heat, heat the brown sugar, butter, half-and-half, and salt to a gentle boil while stirring carefully, 5 to 7 minutes.

2. When the sauce thickens, remove from heat and stir in the vanilla extract.

3. Spoon the sauce over the cheesecake when ready to serve. The sauce will thicken when cooled. Reheat to pour easily.

INGREDIENT TIP: Make sure to grind black sesame seeds only to a coarse powder. When black sesame seeds are ground fine, they can be become bitter. You can also grind the sesame seeds using a mortar and pestle.

Per Serving: Calories: 582; Total fat: 45g; Protein: 12g; Carbs: 37g; Fiber: 3g; Sugar: 21g; Sodium: 423mg

INDONESIAN STEAMED COCONUT CUPCAKE

INDONESIA

Prep time: 15 minutes

Cook time: 1 hour on high

Makes 6 or 7 small cupcakes

These little coconut cupcakes are not only adorable; they are little bites of deliciousness! *Putu Ayu* is a dessert traditionally made with pandan leaves, which release a vibrant green extract when puréed. It is sometimes a challenge to find pandan leaves at the grocery store, so I often resort to using a few drops of food coloring. The slow cooker's ability to steam these cupcakes at a steady temperature gives great results. What's even better is that you don't have to mess with any added oil or butter. I like serving these with sliced mango. I use small individual silicone cupcake molds for this recipe.

Cooking spray

½ cup unsweetened shredded coconut

2 tablespoons water, plus more if needed

Pinch salt (optional)

1 large egg

½ cup sugar

½ cup all-purpose flour

½ teaspoon baking powder

¼ cup plus 2 tablespoons coconut milk

1 to 2 drops green food coloring (optional)

1. Place a rack in the slower cooker. If you don't have a rack, make 6 or 7 aluminum foil balls with an indent in the middle (to hold cupcake molds securely). Make sure the foil balls are ¾ to 1 inch high. Pour hot water to the top of the rack or foil balls. Wrap the slow cooker lid tightly with a kitchen towel, tying the ends up on top, to prevent condensation on the lid from dripping on to the cupcakes. Cover and set on high while you prepare the cupcakes.

2. Spray 6 or 7 standard-size silicone cupcake molds lightly with cooking spray.

3. In a small bowl, combine the coconut, water, and salt, if using, so that the coconut is just moistened. Add a little more water if needed. Set aside.

4. In a medium bowl, using a hand mixer on medium to medium-high speed, beat the egg and sugar together until pale and creamy, about 1 minute.

> **CONTINUED**

Indonesian Steamed Coconut Cupcake

> **CONTINUED**

5. Sift the flour and baking powder into the egg mixture and stir until just combined.

6. Add the coconut milk and green food coloring, if using, to the batter and mix again until combined.

7. In each cupcake mold, layer about 1 spoonful of coconut on the bottom. Press the coconut down until it is firmly packed.

8. Fill the molds with the batter, leaving ¼ inch of space at the top.

9. Place the molds in the slow cooker, cover, and cook on high for 1 hour, or until a toothpick inserted in the center of the cupcakes comes out clean.

10. Remove the cupcakes from the slow cooker and let them rest on a cooling rack for about 5 minutes.

11. Gently turn the cupcakes upside down and release them from the molds. Serve with the coconut layer facing up.

OPTION TIP: If you have access to pandan leaves, for step 6, chop 2 leaves and place them in a blender with the coconut milk, and blend until puréed. Strain the blended coconut milk through a fine-mesh sieve covered with cheesecloth into a bowl, then mix with the batter.

Per Serving: Calories: 268; Total fat: 15g; Protein: 4g; Carbs: 30g; Fiber: 3g; Sugar: 19g; Sodium: 21mg

COCONUT CUSTARD

Prep time: **15 minutes**

Cook time: **2 to 2½ hours on high**

Serves **5 or 6**

SRI LANKA

Watalappan is a creamy coconut custard sweetened with jaggery and spiced with nutmeg and cardamom powder. Jaggery, an unrefined sugar that typically comes from the sap of palm trees, has an almost caramel flavor with deeper notes. You can substitute palm sugar if you cannot find jaggery.

Cooking spray

¾ cup grated jaggery or grated palm sugar

1 cup full-fat coconut milk

¼ teaspoon ground nutmeg

¼ teaspoon cardamom powder

1 teaspoon vanilla extract

4 large eggs

¼ cup unsalted roasted cashews, roughly chopped, for garnish

1. Place a rack or an aluminum foil coil about 2 inches thick in the slow cooker. Pour hot water to the top of the rack or coil. Wrap the slow cooker lid tightly with a kitchen towel, tying the ends up on top, to prevent water from dripping on the custard.

2. Spray a 6-inch round pan or baking dish with cooking spray. Set aside.

3. In a small saucepan over medium-high heat, combine the jaggery, coconut milk, nutmeg, cardamom powder, and vanilla extract. Stir and heat only until the jaggery has melted. Remove from heat and set aside to cool.

4. In a mixing bowl, gently whisk the eggs until they are light and not too frothy. Once the coconut milk mixture has slightly cooled, slowly add it to the eggs while whisking to prevent curdling until combined.

5. Strain the mixture through a fine-mesh sieve into another bowl.

6. Pour the custard mixture into the prepared pan. Using the back of a spoon, smooth down any air bubbles on the surface. Place the pan in the slow cooker.

> **CONTINUED**

Coconut Custard

> **CONTINUED**

7. Cover and cook on high for 2 to 2½ hours, or until the custard is set and the middle has a very slight wobble.

8. Remove from the slow cooker and allow to cool. Cover with plastic wrap and refrigerate until chilled, 3 to 5 hours.

9. Garnish with the chopped cashews and serve.

OPTION TIP: If you prefer, make this custard in individual ramekins instead of a larger baking dish.

SUBSTITUTION TIP: If it is difficult to find jaggery or palm sugar, use ¼ cup light brown sugar.

Per Serving: Calories: 235; Total fat: 19g; Protein: 7g; Carbs: 13g; Fiber: 1g; Sugar: 10g; Sodium: 64mg

ASIAN PEAR UPSIDE-DOWN CAKE

CHINA, JAPAN, KOREA

Prep time: 25 minutes

Cook time: 2 to 2½ hours on high

Serves 6

After dinner, my mother would grab Asian pears, masterfully peel them with a paring knife, slice them, and hand the slices to us one by one. That was dessert for us. I'm such a cake lover that it only seemed natural for me to combine the two. If you love ginger, use up to a teaspoon. Serve this cake with vanilla ice cream or whipped cream.

Cooking spray or butter, for greasing

6 tablespoons unsalted butter, divided

2 tablespoons light brown sugar

1 large Asian pear, peeled, cored, and cut in ½- to ¾-inch-thick slices

1 cup all-purpose flour

1 teaspoon baking powder

1 teaspoon ground cinnamon

½ to 1 teaspoon ground ginger

¼ teaspoon salt

⅔ cup sugar

2 large eggs

1 teaspoon vanilla extract

¼ cup whole milk, divided

1. Place a rack or an aluminum foil coil about 2 inches thick inside the slow cooker. Wrap the slow cooker lid tightly with a kitchen towel, tying the ends up on top, to prevent condensation on the lid.

2. Lightly grease the sides of 6-inch round baking pan, and line the bottom with parchment paper. If you have an oval slow cooker, you could use a 9-by-5-inch loaf pan. Set aside.

3. Cut 2 tablespoons of butter into small cubes. Sprinkle the butter cubes and the brown sugar on the bottom of the prepared pan in an even layer.

4. Add the pear slices in a single layer, overlapping them a little if needed.

5. In a small bowl, whisk the flour, baking powder, cinnamon, ginger, and salt together. Set aside.

6. Soften the remaining 4 tablespoons of butter. In a large mixing bowl, use a hand mixer to beat the sugar and softened butter until blended, about 2 minutes.

7. Add the eggs to the sugar and butter mixture one at a time, beating after each egg. Add the vanilla extract and beat until combined.

> **CONTINUED**

Asian Pear Upside-Down Cake

> **CONTINUED**

8. Add half of the dry mixture to the wet mixture and beat on low speed. Add 2 tablespoons of milk and continue to mix. Repeat with the second half of the dry mixture and remaining 2 tablespoons of milk. Beat the batter on medium speed until all the ingredients have combined and batter is smooth.

9. Spread the batter over the pears, leaving ½ inch of space at the top of the pan. Place the pan in the slow cooker.

10. Cover and cook on high for 2 to 2½ hours, until a toothpick inserted in the middle of the cake comes out clean.

11. Transfer the pan to a cooling rack and let the cake rest for 20 to 30 minutes.

12. Carefully run a paring knife around the edge of the cake. Place a platter or plate on top of cake, flip the cake over, and gently lift the cake pan. Slice and serve.

SUBSTITUTION TIP: If you can't find Asian pears, you can use Bosc pears.

Per Serving: Calories: 327; Total fat: 14g; Protein: 5g; Carbs: 47g; Fiber: 3g; Sugar: 29g; Sodium: 208mg

MANGO COMPOTE

Prep time: **10 minutes**

Cook time: **6 to 7 hours on low, 2 to 3 hours on high**

Serves **8**

INDIA, PHILIPPINES

You'll know when mangoes are in season at our house. We buy quite a few to cut up and store in the fridge so that we can munch on them all week. We also make this Mango Compote in the slow cooker overnight to add to yogurt and toast in the morning. It's also a yummy topping on a big scoop of vanilla ice cream.

Cooking spray

4 mangoes, peeled, seeded, and thinly sliced

¼ cup sugar

3 tablespoons lemon juice

2 tablespoons lime juice

⅛ to ¼ teaspoon ground ginger

1. Spray the slow cooker lightly with cooking spray.

2. In the slow cooker, combine the mangoes, sugar, lemon juice, lime juice, and ginger. Mix well.

3. Cover and cook on low for 6 to 7 hours or on high for 2 to 3 hours.

4. Stir and serve as a topping.

SUBSTITUTION TIP: You can use frozen mangoes if fresh ones are not in season. Use 5 cups of frozen mango.

Per Serving: Calories: 128; Total fat: 1g; Protein: 2g; Carbs: 32g; Fiber: 3g; Sugar: 29g; Sodium: 3mg

STIR-FRIED ASPARAGUS, PAGE 140

9

SIDE DISHES & SALADS

STIR-FRIED ASPARAGUS 140

THAI CUCUMBER RELISH 141

FRESH KIMCHI 142

CARROT SAMBOL 144

TOMATO SALAD 145

GREEN PAPAYA SALAD 146

STIR-FRIED LOTUS ROOT 147

SPICY RADISH SALAD 148

BOK CHOY WITH MUSHROOMS 149

MISO SALAD DRESSING 150

A great advantage that I love about the slow cooker is that it enables me to make multiple dishes with ease. The recipes in this chapter are simple side dishes and salads that can accompany main dishes. None are slow cooked, but you can prepare them while your slow-cooker dish is cooking. You might find a few recipes that can stand on their own, though, like the Green Papaya Salad—it's light and refreshing, and you can add a protein if you like.

STIR-FRIED ASPARAGUS

Prep time: **10 minutes**

Cook time: **5 minutes**

Serves **4 or 5**

CHINA

There's a well-known restaurant in our area where I love ordering the asparagus. Although this isn't the restaurant's recipe, I like whipping up this version at home to go with our meals. It's a great vegetable side dish that is very easy to prepare. This cooks fast in the pan, so make sure to not overcook it.

1½ tablespoons vegetable oil

1 pound asparagus, trimmed and sliced thinly on the bias

½ teaspoon garlic powder

1 tablespoon oyster sauce

¼ teaspoon freshly ground black pepper

Salt

2 teaspoons sesame seeds

1. In a large pan, heat the oil over medium-high heat. Add the asparagus, garlic powder, oyster sauce, and pepper, and stir-fry for about 3 minutes.

2. Season with salt. The asparagus is done when heated through but still crisp. Do not overcook. Sprinkle with sesame seeds and serve immediately.

TECHNIQUE TIP: Cutting the asparagus on the bias allows for fast and even cooking when stir-frying. It also exposes more of the interior flesh to allow more sauce to flavor the asparagus. After trimming the ends, slice the asparagus spears diagonally in 1½-inch to 2-inch lengths.

Per Serving: Calories: 78; Total fat: 6g; Protein: 3g; Carbs: 5g; Fiber: 3g; Sugar: 2g; Sodium: 69mg

THAI CUCUMBER RELISH

Prep time: **15 minutes**

Serves **6**

If you've ever ordered Chicken Satay at a Thai restaurant, chances are it was served with a side of *Ajad*. This cucumber relish is bright, sweet, tart, and slightly spicy. It's a wonderful accompaniment to curries, and you can adjust the spiciness based on however many chiles you want to use.

¼ cup sugar

½ cup white vinegar

½ teaspoon salt

2 tablespoons water

2 cups quartered, thinly sliced cucumber

¼ cup thinly sliced shallots

1 Thai chile, thinly sliced (optional)

2 tablespoons chopped fresh cilantro

1. In a small saucepan, heat the sugar, vinegar, salt, and water together over medium-low heat until the sugar and salt have dissolved, about 1 minute. Set aside to cool to room temperature.

2. In a medium bowl, combine the cucumber, shallots, chile (if using), and cilantro and toss.

3. Once the dressing is cool, pour it over the cucumber mixture and toss well. Set aside for 10 more minutes to let the flavors meld before serving.

PREP IT RIGHT: You can make this side dish up to 3 days in advance. Store refrigerated in an airtight container until ready for use.

Per Serving: Calories: 46; Total fat: 0g; Protein: 0g; Carbs: 11g; Fiber: 0g; Sugar: 9g; Sodium: 196mg

FRESH KIMCHI

Prep time: 45 minutes

Serves **9 or 10**

There are many varieties of kimchi and different ways of making this Korean staple. The fermentation process of many kimchis can take days, but *Baechu Geotjeori* is a kimchi you can make and eat the same day. This kimchi is bright and fresh, and tastes more like a salad compared to its fermented cousin. This isn't really a shortcut method, but it isn't super difficult. A whole napa cabbage makes a lot, so if you want a smaller batch, this recipe can be easily cut in half.

5 cups water, divided

¼ cup mochiko (sweet rice flour)

½ cup sea salt

1 small napa cabbage, 2½ to 3 pounds

1 medium yellow onion, quartered

2-inch piece fresh ginger, peeled and sliced

½ Asian pear, peeled, cored, and quartered

1 cup gochugaru (Korean red pepper flakes)

¼ cup finely minced garlic

¼ cup oligodang (Korean oligosaccharide syrup) or corn syrup

¼ cup fish sauce, plus more if needed

¼ cup sesame seeds

4 scallions, both white and green parts cut into ½-inch lengths

Kosher salt, if needed

1. In a small saucepan, heat 2 cups of water and sweet rice flour over medium heat until it reaches a boil. Continue whisking until the consistency is like pudding. Turn the heat off, set aside, and cool to room temperature. For faster cooling, transfer the mixture to a bowl and refrigerate.

2. Trim the stem off the cabbage. Cut the cabbage in half lengthwise, then cut each half lengthwise into ¼- to ½-inch-wide strips, and place in a very large bowl.

3. Mix the sea salt with the remaining 3 cups of water and stir until the salt is dissolved. Pour the salt water onto the cabbage and let sit for 15 minutes, then turn the cabbage over so that the bottom leaves are now at the top, and let sit for another 15 minutes.

4. Meanwhile, prepare the marinade. Once the rice flour mixture has cooled, transfer it to a blender with the onion, ginger, and Asian pear. Blend until puréed, then transfer to a large bowl.

5. In the bowl, add the gochugaru, garlic, oligodang, fish sauce, sesame seeds, and scallions, and stir until combined. Taste and season with kosher salt if needed, 1 teaspoon at a time, and set aside.

6. Rinse the cabbage under cold water two or three times, drain well, and return to its bowl.

7. Add half of the kimchi marinade to the cabbage and toss until the cabbage leaves are evenly coated. If needed, add more marinade 1 spoonful at a time as you mix the kimchi. Save any leftover marinade in the refrigerator in an airtight container.

8. Taste the kimchi and add more kosher salt or fish sauce if needed. Serve as a side dish with rice.

TECHNIQUE TIP: Since the marinade includes a lot of red pepper flakes, using kitchen gloves when mixing the kimchi can protect your hands.

LEFTOVERS TIP: If you have leftover marinade, use it for another batch of kimchi, or you can cook with it. I have used leftover marinade in stir-fries and in seafood dishes.

Per Serving: Calories: 112; Total fat: 3g; Protein: 5g; Carbs: 21g; Fiber: 3g; Sugar: 7g; Sodium: 1,138mg

CARROT SAMBOL

Prep time: **15 minutes**

Serves **6**

SRI LANKA

Carrot Sambol is simple to make and a wonderful accompaniment to rice and curries. There's a bright flavor from the carrots and lime juice with a hint of spice from green chiles. If we have any left over, I often throw some on a bed of romaine lettuce with a little protein for a complete lunch.

3 cups grated carrots

¾ cup thinly sliced or diced red onion

1 cup finely diced Roma tomatoes

2 to 3 green chiles, finely chopped

⅓ cup unsweetened shredded coconut

¼ cup fresh lime juice

¼ teaspoon salt, plus more if needed

¼ teaspoon freshly ground black pepper, plus more if needed

In a bowl, toss together the carrots, onion, tomatoes, chiles, coconut, lime juice, salt, and pepper. Season with additional salt and pepper, if desired.

OPTION TIP: If you do not like spicy food, you can use a smaller amount of green chiles or omit them.

Per Serving: Calories: 129; Total fat: 8g; Protein: 2g; Carbs: 13g; Fiber: 4g; Sugar: 6g; Sodium: 142mg

TOMATO SALAD

Prep time: 5 minutes, plus 30 minutes to make garlic oil

Cook time: 5 minutes

Serves 6

MYANMAR

Tomato salads are my summer go-to salads. I also like bringing them to potlucks because they tend to hold up better than leafy salads that can wilt. This tomato salad is dressed with a fragrant garlic oil and black sesame seeds, which bring in a nice earthy flavor. If you like more acidity, use a whole lime instead of half.

4 garlic cloves, smashed

½ cup vegetable oil

¼ cup diced red onion

½ cup loosely packed chopped fresh cilantro

2 tablespoons unroasted black sesame seeds, roughly ground

3 tablespoons roasted unsalted peanuts, chopped

Juice of ½ lime

¼ teaspoon salt

¼ teaspoon freshly ground black pepper

5 tomatoes, sliced

1. In a small saucepan, heat the garlic and oil over medium-low heat until the garlic is a little golden but not brown, being careful not to overcook, about 5 minutes.

2. Remove the garlic oil from the heat and allow it to cool to room temperature, about 30 minutes. The garlic will continue to cook and infuse the oil.

3. In a medium bowl, combine the onion, cilantro, sesame seeds, peanuts, lime juice, salt, pepper, and 1½ tablespoons of the cooled garlic oil. Reserve the remaining garlic oil for another use.

4. Arrange the tomatoes in a serving dish and pour the dressing over them. Lightly toss and serve.

INGREDIENT TIP: Roasted black sesame seeds can start to taste bitter when ground, so make sure to use unroasted ones for this salad. If you cannot find black sesame seeds, you can use roasted white sesame seeds.

TIME-SAVING TIP: If you do not want to make your own garlic oil, use any salad oil of your choice.

Per Serving: Calories: 229; Total fat: 22g; Protein: 3g; Carbs: 7g; Fiber: 2g; Sugar: 3g; Sodium: 104mg

GREEN PAPAYA SALAD

Prep time: 20 minutes

Serves 6

VIETNAM

Green papaya is essential to make *Goi Du Du*. Unlike orange papaya, green papaya tastes a bit like cucumber with a firmer texture. The fruit is sold in most Chinese or Southeast Asian markets, although I've been seeing it around more in major grocery stores and farmers' markets. Find a nice shiny one that is firm with smooth outer skin. Seasoned with fish sauce, vinegar, and sugar—playing off salty and sweet flavors—this salad is oil free, light, and refreshing.

1 to 1½ pounds green papaya, peeled, seeded, and julienned

1 carrot, julienned

¼ cup chopped fresh mint leaves

¼ cup chopped fresh cilantro

1 red chile, thinly sliced

¼ cup fish sauce

¼ cup white vinegar

3 tablespoons sugar

½ cup water

¼ cup fried shallots (optional)

¼ cup roasted unsalted peanuts, chopped

1 lime, cut into wedges, for serving

1. In a large bowl, toss together the papaya, carrot, mint, cilantro, and chile.

2. In a separate bowl, combine the fish sauce, vinegar, sugar, and water, and stir until the sugar dissolves.

3. Spoon about half of the dressing over the salad and toss to evenly coat. Add more dressing if needed.

4. Add shallots, if using, and peanuts, and lightly toss. Serve with lime wedges.

TECHNIQUE TIP: A mandoline is very helpful for prepping the papaya and carrot.

Per Serving: Calories: 116; Total fat: 3g; Protein: 4g; Carbs: 21g; Fiber: 5g; Sugar: 8g; Sodium: 946mg

STIR-FRIED LOTUS ROOT

Prep time: **15 minutes**

Cook time: **10 minutes**

Serves **5 or 6**

JAPAN

My family frequently visits an *izakaya* in our area where one of our favorite vegetable dishes is *Kinpira Renkon*, sautéed lotus root. An izakaya is a Japanese pub or drinking establishment that serves small plates of food to be shared. Lotus root has a mild flavor with a crunchy texture similar to celery and is packed with nutrients. In this recipe, the lotus root is sautéed first and then braised in mirin, sake, and soy sauce.

12 ounces lotus root, peeled, quartered lengthwise, and thinly sliced

1 teaspoon white vinegar

3 cups water

2 tablespoons sake

2 tablespoons mirin

1 tablespoon sugar

1 tablespoon vegetable oil

¼ to ½ teaspoon red pepper flakes (optional)

2 tablespoons soy sauce

1 teaspoon sesame oil

1 teaspoon roasted sesame seeds

1. In a medium bowl, soak the lotus root in the vinegar and water for about 5 minutes.

2. Meanwhile, in a small bowl, mix the sake, mirin, and sugar.

3. Drain the lotus root well.

4. In a large pan, heat the oil over medium heat and add the lotus root. Sauté until the lotus root turns almost translucent, about 3 minutes.

5. Add the sake-mirin mixture, and stir. Cook until the liquid is almost gone, about 2 minutes.

6. Add the pepper flakes (if using), soy sauce, and sesame oil, stirring continuously to prevent burning. Cook until the liquid is almost gone, 1 to 2 minutes, then remove from heat.

7. Sprinkle with sesame seeds and serve.

TECHNIQUE TIP: Soaking the lotus root in water with a little bit of vinegar helps prevent it from turning brown. This process isn't necessary for flavor, so you can bypass this step if you want.

Per Serving: Calories: 98; Total fat: 3g; Protein: 2g; Carbs: 15g; Fiber: 3g; Sugar: 3g; Sodium: 367mg

SPICY RADISH SALAD

Prep time: 15 minutes

Serves 6

Musaengchae is spicy, fresh, healthy, and the perfect topping for Korean Pork Wraps (page 109). It's also a great *banchan* (side dish) to many meals.

1 pound Korean radish, peeled and cut into matchsticks

2 teaspoons sea salt

2 scallions, thinly sliced

1 tablespoon minced garlic

1 tablespoon sesame seeds

2 teaspoons fish sauce

3 to 4 tablespoons gochugaru (Korean red chili flakes)

1 to 2 teaspoons sugar

1. Place the radishes in a large bowl. Sprinkle with the salt and stir to coat evenly. Set aside for 5 minutes.

2. In a small bowl, combine the scallions, garlic, sesame seeds, fish sauce, gochugaru, and sugar.

3. Drain the radish. Gently squeeze to remove any excess water.

4. Add the spice mixture to the radish and mix well with your hands. Serve.

INGREDIENT TIP: Most gochugaru and fish sauces are naturally gluten-free, but double-check the ingredient labels to make sure. Some gochugaru is spicier than others. If you want to cut the heat a little, add a bit more sugar.

SUBSTITUTION TIP: If you cannot find Korean radish, you can use daikon.

TIME-SAVING TIP: Use a mandoline slicer to cut the radish.

Per Serving: Calories: 33; Total fat: 1g; Protein: 1g; Carbs: 6g; Fiber: 2g; Sugar: 3g; Sodium: 810mg

BOK CHOY WITH MUSHROOMS

CHINA

Prep time: **10 minutes**

Cook time: **10 minutes**

Serves **4 or 5**

This stir-fry is fast and simple to make and goes well as a quick side to a main dish. This dish is usually served with the vegetables whole, not sliced, and with the bok choy and mushrooms separated. However, this version offers a great option for those who want bite sizes.

2 tablespoons vegetable oil

1 tablespoon minced garlic

8 to 10 shiitake mushrooms, stemmed and halved

1 pound bok choy, cut into 1- to 1½-inch pieces

2 tablespoons oyster sauce

1 teaspoon sesame oil

1. In a large pan, heat the vegetable oil over medium-high heat.

2. Add the garlic and fry until fragrant, about 20 seconds.

3. Add the mushrooms and stir-fry for 1 minute.

4. Add the bok choy, oyster sauce, and sesame oil, and stir-fry for another 1 to 2 minutes, making sure the greens are still bright and tender and not overcooked. Remove from heat and serve.

SUBSTITUTION TIP: If you cannot find shiitake mushrooms, use cremini mushrooms instead.

Per Serving: Calories: 96; Total fat: 8g; Protein: 2g; Carbs: 5g; Fiber: 2g; Sugar: 2g; Sodium: 131mg

MISO SALAD DRESSING

Prep time: **10 minutes**

Makes **1 cup**

JAPAN

This salad dressing is very simple to make. White miso is a fermented soybean paste that is lighter in flavor compared to yellow or red miso. It lends itself well to light sauces and salad dressings. This savory dressing is not too sweet, but you can certainly add some honey or sugar if you like. Use it over a bed of your favorite greens, and maybe even add some sliced radish, carrots, cabbage, and edamame.

¼ cup white miso

⅓ cup seasoned rice vinegar

2 tablespoons lime juice

1 teaspoon peeled, grated
fresh ginger

2 tablespoons sesame oil

2 tablespoons extra-virgin
olive oil

In a bowl, whisk the miso, vinegar, lime juice, ginger, sesame oil, and olive oil together until well combined. Serve over salad greens.

OPTION TIP: For a sweeter dressing, add some honey or sugar to taste.

Per Serving (2 tablespoons): Calories: 82; Total fat: 7g; Protein: 1g; Carbs: 3g; Fiber: 1g; Sugar: 1g; Sodium: 360mg

MEASUREMENT & CONVERSION TABLES

Volume Equivalents (Liquid)

Standard	US Standard (ounces)	Metric (approximate)
2 tablespoons	1 fl. oz.	30 mL
¼ cup	2 fl. oz.	60 mL
½ cup	4 fl. oz.	120 mL
1 cup	8 fl. oz.	240 mL
1½ cups	12 fl. oz.	355 mL
2 cups or 1 pint	16 fl. oz.	475 mL
4 cups or 1 quart	32 fl. oz.	1 L
1 gallon	128 fl. oz.	4 L

Volume Equivalents (Dry)

Standard	Metric (approximate)
⅛ teaspoon	0.5 mL
¼ teaspoon	1 mL
½ teaspoon	2 mL
¾ teaspoon	4 mL
1 teaspoon	5 mL
1 tablespoon	15 mL
¼ cup	59 mL
⅓ cup	79 mL
½ cup	118 mL
⅔ cup	156 mL
¾ cup	177 mL
1 cup	235 mL
2 cups or 1 pint	475 mL
3 cups	700 mL
4 cups or 1 quart	1 L

Oven Temperatures

Fahrenheit (F)	Celsius (C) (approximate)
250°	120°
300°	150°
325°	165°
350°	180°
375°	190°
400°	200°
425°	220°
450°	230°

Weight Equivalents

Standard	Metric (approximate)
½ ounce	15 g
1 ounce	30 g
2 ounces	60 g
4 ounces	115 g
8 ounces	225 g
12 ounces	340 g
16 ounces or 1 pound	455 g

ASIAN PANTRY

INGREDIENT	DESCRIPTION	COUNTRY
Bagoong alamang	Bagoong alamang is a Filipino shrimp paste made of fermented shrimp (krill) and salt. It is salty and very pungent. It is used in cooking and as a condiment.	PHILIPPINES
Basmati rice	An aromatic rice with long and slender grains. It is delicate in flavor and is the popular rice of choice in Indian cuisine. Basmati rice can be found in most major grocery stores.	INDIA
Belacan	A dried, pungent, dark brown, fermented shrimp paste used in many Southeast Asian cuisines. It is used in many curry recipes, and powerful in flavor and in smell. Only a small quantity is necessary because it is salty and very pungent. Belacan adds a very savory flavor and depth to dishes. You can find belacan in Asian grocery stores or online. If you cannot find belacan or dried shrimp paste, you can use shrimp paste.	SOUTHEAST ASIA
Bok choy	A hardy type of Chinese cabbage that has a crisp white stalk with green leafy ends.	CHINA (CHINA/TAIWAN)
Buna-Shimeji mushrooms (Bunapi mushrooms)	These mushrooms should always be cooked. They are light and mild in flavor, and hold their texture after cooking.	JAPAN
Cardamom pods and powder	Seed pods that can be used whole or ground that come in green or black pods. It is commonly used in South Asian cuisine and combines a strong aromatic taste with a bittersweet flavor. Usually, it is more common to find recipes that call for green cardamom, and they have a spicy and sweet taste. Because of this, it is used in savory as well as sweet dishes.	INDIA

INGREDIENT	DESCRIPTION	COUNTRY
Chinese black vinegar	A dark vinegar that is primarily made with rice and sometimes with wheat and barley. It is common in Chinese cooking. This vinegar is strong and fragrant, and although it is tart, it is also slightly sweet. If you cannot find Chinese black vinegar, the closest substitute is balsamic vinegar. However, balsamic vinegar is a little sweeter than black vinegar, so you may have to cut down on any sugar if the recipe calls for sugar.	CHINA (CHINA/TAIWAN)
Chinese five-spice powder	A spice blend from five spices generally used for stir-fries and marinades. The most common spices used are cinnamon, cloves, fennel, star anise, and Szechuan peppercorns. Can be found in most major grocery stores.	CHINA (CHINA/TAIWAN)
Coconut milk	The liquid that has been extracted from the grated meat of a coconut. This creamy and rich milk is usually found in cans at most major grocery stores.	SOUTHEAST AND SOUTH ASIA
Coconut water	The liquid that is found inside young coconuts. It is clear, light, and slightly sweet.	SOUTHEAST AND SOUTH ASIA
Coriander powder	A sweet and citrusy spice, coriander powder is made from ground coriander seeds. It is used in many Indian recipes, and can be found in most major grocery stores.	INDIA
Cumin	Seeds that are used ground or whole. It is common to find cumin in Indian cuisine (along with Mexican and Middle Eastern cuisine), and has an aromatic and nutty flavor. Cumin is used in many spice blends and is used in curries, stews, and marinades. It can be found in most major grocery stores.	INDIA

INGREDIENT	DESCRIPTION	COUNTRY
Curry leaves	Curry leaves are not to be confused with curry powder. Curry leaves are dark green, small, and have a similar shape to lemon leaves. They have citrus notes with a bitter and slightly sweet taste. There's no good substitute for curry leaves, but you can try using a dry bay leaf. Otherwise, omit them from the recipe if you cannot get access to any. They can be found in Indian and Asian markets and are also available online.	INDIA/SRI LANKA
Curry powder	A mix of spices that can come in a variety of blends. Most contain turmeric, coriander, fenugreek, cumin, and black pepper. However, I like using the S&B brand, which has about sixteen spices in its blend, and it can be found in Asian grocery stores or online.	
Curry sauce mix (blocks)	Japanese curry sauce mix is a premade curry roux that come in blocks. It can be found in most major grocery stores and Asian grocery stores.	JAPAN
Dangmyeon	Made from sweet potato starch, these translucent Korean vermicelli noodles are glassy and a little chewy. Dangmyeon is used in stir-fries and soups. Can be found in Korean markets, Asian grocery stores, and online.	KOREA
Dark soy sauce	Aged for a longer period of time with molasses, dark soy sauce is thicker and darker in color. It is slightly sweet and is used in many marinades and stir-fries.	CHINA (CHINA/TAIWAN)
Dashi stock	Dashi is a Japanese soup stock that is made from water, bonito fish flakes, and kombu (dried kelp). This clear broth is simple to make by combining the three ingredients and simmering for ten to twenty minutes. Dashi is fundamental to Japanese cuisine, and enhances savory flavors in dishes. You can also find this soup stock in a powder form and simply add it to water.	JAPAN

INGREDIENT	DESCRIPTION	COUNTRY
Doenjang	Korean fermented soybean paste that has deep, bold, rich, and savory flavors from months of fermentation. The paste is not smooth, but rather coarse in texture. Doenjang is used in many soups, marinades, and dipping sauces. You can find doenjang at many Asian markets and online.	KOREA
Doubanjiang	Used in many Chinese Sichuan (Szechuan) cuisines, this bean paste is made from fermented broad beans (fava beans), salt, and spices.	CHINA (CHINA/ TAIWAN)
Dried lotus leaves	Large leaves from the aquatic lotus plant. Usually used to wrap food and cooked to add aromatic tones to the dish. Dried lotus leaves are a little less potent and give a more earthy aroma.	CHINA, THAI
Dried red chile peppers	Whole Chinese or Thai red chile peppers that have been dried.	NORTH, SOUTHEAST ASIA
Fennel, seeds and ground	Fennel seeds and ground fennel are used in many parts of the world. Fennel is aromatic and perfume-like with anise and licorice flavors.	INDIA
Fermented black beans	Known as Douchi, these fermented salted black soybeans are commonly used in Chinese cuisine. They come whole and add deep salty flavors that are similar to soy sauce, but a saltier and sharper flavor.	CHINA (CHINA/ TAIWAN)
Fish sauce	Made from salted fermented fish, this light brown salty sauce is primarily used in East and Southeast Asian cuisine. It is becoming more and more common to find fish sauce in major grocery retailers.	COMMON
Galangal	Galangal and ginger are a part of the same ginger family, but both taste different from each other. Galangal has a strong earthy flavor, with citrusy notes. It has a pale and thin skin, with a tough flesh, and it becomes tougher with age. It is used in many Southeast Asian cuisines for soups, stews, and pounded into a paste for curries.	NORTH, SOUTH, SOUTHEAST ASIA

INGREDIENT	DESCRIPTION	COUNTRY
Garam masala	A spice blend that is used in a lot of Indian cuisine. Some of the common spices used in this blend are bay leaves, black peppercorns, cardamom pods, carom seeds, cinnamon, cloves, coriander, cumin, and mace. The spices are roasted before being ground, and although it is used during the cooking process, garam masala is typically added at the end of cooking to enhance flavors. You can usually find garam masala in the spice aisle at major grocery stores.	INDIA
Ginger	Widely used in Asian cuisine, ginger root has a soft skin with a pale yellow flesh. Ginger is very fragrant and mildly spicy, but is less pungent and sweeter than galangal.	COMMON
Ginseng	The ginseng root has a very earthy aroma and flavor. It is quite aromatic and tastes sour and bitter. Ginseng is used in beverages, traditional Chinese medicine, and as an ingredient in dishes.	NORTH ASIA AND SOME SOUTHEAST ASIAN COUNTRIES
Gochugaru	Korean red chili pepper flakes made from dried, deseeded Korean chiles. Gochugaru varies in heat level, from mild to spicy, can be coarsely or finely ground. It is a staple in Korean cuisine. Once the package is opened, store gochugaru in an airtight bag or container in the freezer to maintain freshness and color.	KOREA
Gochujang	Korean red chili paste that is typically made with chili powder, fermented soybean powder, glutinous sweet rice powder, and salt. Gochujang is thick, spicy, slightly pungent, and sweet. It is a versatile ingredient used in many different ways—soups, stews, marinades, sauces, and stir-fries. This fiery sauce can come in various spice levels and is a staple in Korean cuisine.	KOREA

INGREDIENT	DESCRIPTION	COUNTRY
Green papaya	A green papaya is an immature unripened papaya with a white flesh. It is very mild in flavor and is crunchy, unlike a soft ripened orange papaya. It reminds me most of cucumber and can be found in Southeast Asian grocery stores. I have been seeing it around more at major grocery stores and farmers' markets.	SOUTHEAST ASIA
Hoisin	Commonly used in Chinese cuisine, Hoisin is also a popular condiment in Vietnam. The sauce is dark, thick, salty, sour, and slightly sweet. It is used in many marinades, stir-fries, and as a dipping sauce. Hoisin can be found in most major grocery stores.	CHINA (CHINA/ TAIWAN)
Jaggery	Jaggery is an unrefined sugar that typically comes from the sap of palm trees. The result is a golden, almost caramel-y flavor with deeper notes. You can substitute palm sugar if you cannot find jaggery in the store or online.	INDIA/SRI LANKA/ SOUTHEAST ASIA
Jjajang	Fermented black bean paste that is roasted and commonly used for Jjajangmyeon. It is dark, savory, and has a slight caramel flavor.	KOREA
Jujubes	Chinese red dates. The dried dates are not overly sweet, and are used for cooking and to flavor beverages.	NORTH AND SOUTH ASIA
Kaffir lime leaves	Used in many Southeast Asian dishes, kaffir lime leaves add bright citrus flavors to dishes. It can be sliced and eaten raw (especially the lighter and younger leaves) in salads, and cooked in curries and soups. Kaffir lime leaves can be found in Southeast Asian grocery stores or online. If you get a big batch, they can be stored in the freezer. If you have trouble finding these, you can use lime peels.	SOUTHEAST ASIA
Karashi	A yellow Japanese hot mustard used as a condiment and seasoning. It is very hot and spicy, and not tangy and sour like Western yellow mustard. Karashi is often used in dipping sauces and usually comes in a powder form. To use Karashi, add a little bit of warm water to make into a paste.	JAPAN

INGREDIENT	DESCRIPTION	COUNTRY
Kashmiri chili powder	A vibrantly red chili powder made from Kashmiri chiles, and used to add color and some heat to dishes. On the spice scale, it is hotter than paprika and milder than cayenne. If you cannot find Kashmiri chili powder, you can substitute it by using a three-to-one ratio of paprika to cayenne.	INDIA
Kecap manis	Indonesian sweet soy sauce that is syrupy, dark, and thick. It is a soy sauce that has been sweetened with palm sugar, and it is a popular ingredient in Indonesian cuisine. Kecap manis is used in marinades, stir-fries, grilled meats, and also as a dipping sauce.	INDONESIA
Kimchi	Kimchi is made of vegetables that are seasoned, brined, and fermented. There are many different varieties of kimchi that can encompass flavors that are spicy, tangy, sweet, and sour. Kimchi can stand on its own as a side dish, but can also be used in soups, stews, and stir-fries. You can find kimchi in Korean markets and Asian markets, and I've been seeing it more and more in major grocery stores.	KOREA
Laksa paste	A curry paste that is used for laksa, a Singaporean and Malaysian noodle soup. Dried chiles, lemongrass, onion, garlic, galangal, turmeric, and dried shrimp paste are common ingredients found in laksa paste. You can find premade laksa paste in Asian grocery stores or online.	SINGAPORE/ MALAYSIA
Lemongrass	A fragrant grass that adds lemon and citrus flavors to dishes. The pale yellow and white parts of the stalk are used for cooking.	SOUTHEAST ASIA
Light soy sauce	Thinner than soy sauce, a light soy sauce is a little saltier and lighter in color. Also, it is not sweet like dark soy sauce.	

INGREDIENT	DESCRIPTION	COUNTRY
Matcha	A finely ground powder made from green tea leaves traditionally used for tea. But this bright and vibrant green powder is also used in desserts and other beverages. Matcha should taste rich in flavor, a bit vegetal, and fresh. There should be a slight sweetness and although it may have a moderate amount of bitterness, it should not be unpleasantly bitter.	JAPAN
Mirin	Commonly used in Japanese cooking, mirin is made from fermented rice. It is similar to sake, but contains more sugar and has a lower alcohol content. Mirin tastes sweet, a little tangy, and is aromatic. It can be found in most Asian markets and online. If you cannot find mirin, you can substitute it by adding a little sugar to dry sherry or a dry white wine.	JAPAN
Miso	Fermented soybean paste used in Japanese cuisine. Miso is thick, and has savory and earthy flavors. Dependent on the fermentation process and age, miso comes in different varieties (like white, yellow, and red), which have tastes that are unique from each other.	JAPAN
Mochiko (glutinous sweet rice flour)	Sweet rice flour is different than white rice flour, so make sure you get the right kind. It is ground from short-grain glutinous rice, and used in baking and as a thickener.	JAPAN
Mu (Korean radish)	A large white radish that has an outer pale green shade near the top. It tastes a little peppery and sweet, and quite dense. Unlike daikon, mu is shorter and more round. But if you cannot find Korean radish (mu), then you can substitute with daikon.	KOREA
Mung bean threads	Thin transparent noodles that are made from mung bean starch.	SOUTHEAST ASIA
Myeolchi	Dried anchovies that come in various sizes. Smaller dried anchovies are typically used for side dishes, whereas larger ones are used for making anchovy broth.	KOREA

INGREDIENT	DESCRIPTION	COUNTRY
Oligodang	Oligodang is oligosaccharide. It is made from corn starch and is thick and syrupy. It is used as a sweetener and can be found in Korean grocery stores or online. If you cannot find oligodang, you can substitute with corn syrup.	KOREA
Oyster sauce	Although it originated in China, oyster sauce is used throughout Asia. It is a dark, thick, and salty sauce with a slightly briny flavor from oysters. Most groceries stores carry oyster sauce, or you can find it at an Asian grocery store or online. There are vegetarian versions of oyster sauce available at specialty grocery stores or online.	CHINA, THAI, VIETNAMESE, CAMBODIA
Palm sugar	An unrefined sugar that typically comes from the sap of palm trees and is used as a sweetener in many Southeast Asian and South Asian cuisine. It has caramel flavor undertones and usually comes in block form (although you can find it in granular and liquid form as well). Palm sugar can be found in most Southeast Asian and South Asian grocery stores or online.	SOUTHEAST AND SOUTH ASIA
Patis	Patis is a fish sauce used in the Philippines, and is a by-product of Bagoong, a fish paste. It is used as a cooking ingredient, in dipping sauces, and as a condiment.	PHILIPPINES
Pechay	Also known as Chinese chard or bok choy, pechay is used a lot in Filipino cuisine and is high in nutrients. It is a type of cabbage where the stalk is crisp and white with green leafy ends.	PHILIPPINES
Pickled mustard greens	Mustard greens that are pickled in a brine and can include various spices in the pickling process. Pickled mustard greens are used as a side dish, condiment, and used in soups and stews. It is a little sour with a slight crunchy texture.	CHINA (CHINA/ TAIWAN/ SOUTHEAST ASIA)
Prahok	Fermented fish paste used in Cambodian cuisine, which is pungent and quite strong in flavor. If you cannot find prahok, you can try substituting with shrimp sauce.	CAMBODIA

INGREDIENT	DESCRIPTION	COUNTRY
Red curry paste	A versatile paste that is commonly made with dried red chiles, shallots, lemongrass, galangal, garlic, shrimp paste, and various spices. Premade Thai red curry pastes are found in most major grocery stores.	THAI
Rice noodles	Noodles made from rice flour and water. They can be found in many major grocery stores.	EAST AND SOUTHEAST ASIA
Saba bananas	Saba bananas are widely used in the Philippines, and although you can eat them raw, they are primarily used for cooking because of their starchy flesh. Saba bananas are shorter and stockier. They are about 4 to 5 inches long and 2 inches in diameter with angles in a rectangular shape. If you cannot find saba bananas, you can substitute them with plantains.	PHILIPPINES
Sake	Sake is a Japanese alcoholic beverage made from fermented rice. In cooking, it is used in many dishes like marinades, stir-fries, grilled foods, soups, and sauces. It can be found in most major grocery stores. If you cannot find sake, you can use a dry white wine.	JAPAN
Sambal oelek	A hot sauce made primarily of chili peppers and salt. There are some versions that use garlic, vinegar, onion, and lime or lemon juice.	SOUTHEAST ASIA
Seasoned rice vinegar	A rice vinegar that is sweeter and less acidic than regular rice vinegar. It is often used for dressings and dipping sauces.	EAST AND SOUTHEAST ASIA
Sesame oil	Extracted from toasted sesame seeds, this oil is used in cooking and as a flavor enhancer at the end of cooking. It has a nutty and earthy fragrance, and a little goes a long way. Can be found in major grocery stores.	EAST AND SOUTHEAST ASIA
Shaoxing wine	Fermented rice wine that is light brown in color and used as a beverage and commonly used in Chinese cuisine. It is similar to dry sherry, which can be used as a substitute, and a little goes a long way.	CHINA (CHINA/TAIWAN)

INGREDIENT	DESCRIPTION	COUNTRY
Shichimi	A Japanese spice blend used for seasoning. The most common ingredients in this blend are red chili pepper, sesame seeds, ground ginger, dried tangerine peel, nori flakes, poppy seeds, and garlic.	JAPAN
Sichuan peppercorns	Sichuan (Szechuan) peppercorns are a common spice used in Chinese cuisine. They are not spicy hot, and instead give a light numbing and tingling sensation. These peppercorns are very fragrant and have a citrusy flavor.	CHINA (CHINA/TAIWAN)
Soy sauce	An essential ingredient in East and Southeast Asian cuisine, soy sauce is made from fermented soybeans, a roasted grain, and salt. There are different varieties of soy sauce ranging in sweetness and from light to dark. Soy sauce can be found in most grocery stores.	EAST AND SOUTHEAST ASIA
Sriracha	A spicy Vietnamese hot sauce that is made from red chiles, vinegar, garlic, sugar, and salt. It is used most as a dipping sauce or a condiment.	VIETNAM
Star anise	A star-shaped dried seed pod that adds a sweet, spicy, and licorice-like flavor to dishes. It can come whole or ground, and is commonly found in Chinese five-spice blends.	CHINA, VIETNAM
Steamed white buns	Steamed white buns are popular in Chinese and Taiwanese cuisine. The dough is mainly made of flour, yeast, and a little sugar, and is steamed. Steamed buns are often stuffed with a protein inside.	CHINA (CHINA/TAIWAN)
Sticky rice (sweet rice)	Sticky rice is also called glutinous or sweet rice, and just like the name says, it has a sticky texture. Although it is also called glutinous rice, it has no gluten in it. Rather, the name refers to it being sticky and glue-like.	CHINA, KOREA, THAI

INGREDIENT	DESCRIPTION	COUNTRY
Tamarind paste	A paste made from the tamarind fruit. It is tart, sour, and citrusy. Ready-made pastes can be found in Southeast Asian markets or online. If you cannot find tamarind paste, you can use lemon or lime juice.	SOUTHEAST ASIA, SOUTH ASIA
Tamarind water	Tamarind water is less concentrated than tamarind paste, and is diluted with water. You can make tamarind water by using 2 teaspoons of tamarind paste mixed with ⅓ cup water.	SOUTHEAST ASIA, SOUTH ASIA
Thai basil	Commonly used in Southeast Asia, Thai basil has smaller and narrower leaves compared to sweet basil. It has a purple stem, and has a licorice-like flavor. This herb also has a more robust flavor with hints of anise. If you cannot access Thai basil, you can use sweet basil.	THAI
Thai chile or Thai bird's eye chile	Small red and green chiles that are very, very hot. These little chiles pack a punch, and they are spicier than jalapeños. Deseeding these chiles can lessen the heat.	SOUTHEAST ASIA, SOME PARTS OF SOUTH ASIA
Tonkatsu sauce	A savory Japanese condiment that is also a little sweet and tangy. The most common ingredients in tonkatsu sauce are ketchup, Worcestershire, soy sauce, and sugar.	JAPAN
Turmeric	A plant from the ginger family, turmeric has an orange-yellow flesh that is a key ingredient to curries and many Asian dishes. Once in powder form, turmeric has an earthy aroma that is musky and slightly bitter. The bright orange-yellow color is unmistakable, and the powder can be found in most major grocery stores.	INDIA
Wood ear mushrooms	A brown fungus that is very mild in flavor. It does not have a spongy soft texture like most mushrooms, nor does it expel a lot of water. Instead, it has a soft crunchy texture which adds a great textural element to dishes.	CHINA (CHINA/TAIWAN)

REFERENCES

Agrawal, Chitra. "Whole Yellow Peas Curry." *The ABCD's of Cooking: Indian Recipes Grown in Brooklyn*. May 6, 2013. http://www.abcdsofcooking.com/2013/05/whole-yellow-peas-curry/.

Amy + Jacky Pressure Cook Recipes (blog). "Instant Pot Three Cup Chicken (San Bei Ji)." February 14, 2017. http://www.pressurecookrecipes.com/instant-pot-three-cup-chicken/.

Amy + Jacky Pressure Cook Recipes (blog). "Pressure Cooker Beef Curry (Japanese)." October 21, 2016. http://www.pressurecookrecipes.com/pressure-cooker-beef-curry-japanese/.

Arsana, Lother, and Heinz von Holzen. *The Food of Indonesia: Delicious Recipes from Bali, Java and the Spice Islands*. Rutland, VT: Tuttle, 2006.

Asian Recipe (blog). "Cambodian (Khmer) Ingredients." Accessed January 24, 2018. http://www.asian-recipe.com/cambodia/cambodian-khmer-ingredients.html.

Asian Recipe (blog). "Indonesian Ingredients." Accessed January 23, 2018. http://www.asian-recipe.com/ingredients/indonesian-ingredients.html.

Chang, Jae-ok. *Vignette of Korean Cooking*. Daegu, Korea: Maeilwonsaek Press, 2000.

Chin, Katie. *Katie Chin's Everyday Chinese Cookbook: 101 Delicious Recipes from My Mother's Kitchen*. Rutland, VT: Tuttle, 2016.

Ellawala, Niranjala M., and Prakash K. Sivanathan. *Sri Lanka the Cookbook*. London: Frances Lincoln, 2017.

Fernando, S. H. *Rice & Curry: Sri Lankan Home Cooking*. New York: Hippocrene Books, 2011.

Ghotra, Hari. *The Easy Indian Slow Cooker Cookbook: Prep-and-Go Restaurant Favorites to Make at Home*. Berkeley, CA: Rockridge Press, 2017.

Jones, Gwen. "Crock Pot Tips, Tricks & Other Cool Stuff." Slow Cooker Kitchen. Accessed January 5, 2018. http://www.slowcookerkitchen.com/crock-pot-tips-tricks-hacks/.

Joo, Judy. *Korean Food Made Simple*. Boston: Houghton Mifflin Harcourt, 2016.

Kitchen, Leanne. "Shan Noodles (Khaut Sew)." *SBS Food*. Accessed January 9, 2018. http://www.sbs.com.au/food/recipes/shan-noodles-khaut-sew.

Kwak, Jenny. *Dok Suni: Recipes From My Mother's Korean Kitchen*. New York: St. Martin's Press, 1998.

Lymm, Joanne. "Savoury Steamed Egg Chawanmushi." *Taiwan Duck*. Accessed February 11, 2018. http://www.taiwanduck.com/savoury-steamed-egg-chawanmushi/.

Maehashi, Yumiko. "Easy Japanese Ramen Noodles." *RecipeTin Japan*. September 19, 2017. http://www.japan.recipetineats.com/easy-japanese-ramen-noodles/.

Maehashi, Yumiko. "Japanese Dressings." *RecipeTin Japan*. August 6, 2016. http://www.japan.recipetineats.com/japanese-dressings/.

Nakry, Mylinh. "Cham-hoy Moan Nung Tirk Doung Chei." *Khmer Krom Recipes*. Accessed February 15, 2018. http://www.khmerkromrecipes.com/recipes/recipe451.html.

O'Dea, Stephanie. "Cooking Marinated Meat in the CrockPot." *A Year of Slow Cooking*. April 22, 2008. http://www.ayearofslowcooking.com/2008/04/cooking-marinated-meat-in-crockpot.html.

Rushton, Joanna. "Slow-Cooked Lamb Kashmir Shanks." *SBS Food*. Accessed February 21, 2018. http://www.sbs.com.au/food/recipes/slow-cooked-lamb-kashmir-shanks.

Solomon, Charmaine. *The Complete Asian Cookbook Series*. Richmond, Australia: Hardie Grant Books, 1976, 2011.

Spices Inc. "List of Spices, Seasonings and Herbs." Accessed February 7, 2018. https://www.spicesinc.com/t-list-of-spices.aspx#Spices.

Tan, Christopher, and Terry Tan. *Singapore Cooking: Fabulous Recipes from Asia's Food Capital*. Rutland, VT: Tuttle, 2009.

Zhu, Maggie. "Authentic Hot and Sour Soup." *Omnivore's Cookbook*. Accessed January 14, 2018. http://www.omnivorescookbook.com/recipes/authentic-hot-and-sour-soup.

RECIPE INDEX

A

Asian Pear Upside-Down
  Cake, 135–136

B

Beef Kare Raisu from
  Scratch, 52–53
Beef Nilaga, 36
Beef Pho Noodle Soup, 30–31
Beef Rendang, 61–62
Beef Short Rib Soup, 24–25
Belacan Not-Fried Chicken, 88
Black Bean Sauce Noodles, 15
Black Sesame
  Cheesecake, 129–130
Black Sticky Rice Pudding, 126
Bok Choy with Mushrooms, 149
Braised Lamb Shanks, 113–114
Braised Pork Belly, 117–118
Braised Pork Shoulder, 104
Braised Short Ribs, 102
Brisket Banh Mi, 119–120
Burmese Chili Chicken, 97

C

Cambodian Caramelized
  Pork, 105
Carrot Sambol, 144
Chicken Adobo, 82
Chicken Arroz Caldo, 12
Chicken Congee, 10
Chicken Devil Curry, 59–60
Chicken Kare Raisu, 54
Chicken Kurma, 64–65
Chicken Lo Mein, 18
Chicken Teriyaki, 98
Chicken Tikka Masala, 49–50
Chinese Five-Spice Whole
  Chicken, 84–85

Chinese Flank Steak &
  Onions, aka Mongolian
  Beef, 103
Chinese-Style "Roasted"
  Lamb, 108
Coconut Custard, 133–134

D

Drunken Noodles, 17

E

Eggplant & Thai Basil, 71
Eggplant Sambal, 78

F

Filipino Chicken Curry, 56
Filipino Oxtail Peanut
  Stew, 37–38
Fresh Kimchi, 142–143

G

Ginger Chicken, 89
Green Papaya Salad, 146

H

Hainanese Chicken Rice, 90–91
Hot-and-Sour Soup, 35

I

Indonesian Braised Tofu, 79
Indonesian Steamed Coconut
  Cupcake, 131–132

K

Kerala Thattukada Chicken, 96
Khmer Curry, 63

Kimchi Stew, 39–40
Korean Ginseng Chicken
  Soup, 27–28
Korean Oxtail Soup, 22–23
Korean Pork Wraps, 109–110

L

Laksa Noodle Soup, 43
Lamb Rogan Josh, 48
Laotian Chicken with
  Mushrooms, 99
Lentil Soup, 34

M

Malaysian Chicken Wings, 83
Mango Compote, 137
Mapo Tofu, 68–69
Matcha & Coconut Mochi
  Cake, 124–125
Miso Salad Dressing, 150
Mushroom Jook, 11

P

Pork Belly Curry, 57–58
Pumpkin Soup, 29

R

Red Chicken Curry, 51
Red Lentil Curry, 55
Roast Chicken, 92

S

Shan Noodles, 19
Shoyu Pork Ramen, 41–42
Simmered Pumpkin, 72
Soybean Paste Stew, 32–33
Soy Silken Tofu, 73
Spiced Cauliflower & Potatoes, 70

Spiced Potatoes, 74
Spicy Baby Back Pork Ribs, 121
Spicy Chickpeas &
     Potatoes, 77
Spicy Lemongrass Chicken, 93
Spicy Radish Salad, 148
Steamed Chicken in Coconut
     Water, 94–95
Steamed Egg with Mushroom &
     Asparagus, 75–76
Sticky Rice in Lotus Leaf, 13–14

Stir-Fried Asparagus, 140
Stir-Fried Lotus Root, 147
Sweet-and-Sour Ribs, 115–116
Sweet Rice Punch, 127–128

T

Taiwanese Braised Pork Belly
     Buns, 106–107
Thai Cucumber Relish, 141
Three-Cup Chicken, 86–87

Tomato Salad, 145
Tom Kha Gai, 26

V

Vietnamese Beef Stew, 44–45
Vietnamese Meatloaf, 111–112

Y

Yellow Mung Beans & Rice, 16

INDEX

A

Almonds
    Chicken Kurma, 64–65
Anaheim chiles
    Burmese Chili Chicken, 97
Asian cuisine
    benefits of slow cooking, 2–3
    flavor map by country, 4–5
    pantry ingredients, 154–165
Asian pears
    Asian Pear Upside-Down
        Cake, 135–136
    Braised Short Ribs, 102
    Fresh Kimchi, 142–143
Asparagus
    Steamed Egg with Mushroom
        & Asparagus, 75–76
    Stir-Fried Asparagus, 140

B

Bagoong alamang, 154
    Filipino Oxtail Peanut
        Stew, 37–38
Bamboo shoots
    Hot-and-Sour Soup, 35
Basmati rice, 154
    Yellow Mung Beans & Rice, 16
Beef. See also Oxtails
    Beef Kare Raisu from
        Scratch, 52–53
    Beef Nilaga, 36
    Beef Pho Noodle
        Soup, 30–31
    Beef Rendang, 61–62
    Beef Short Rib Soup, 24–25
    Braised Short Ribs, 102
    Brisket Banh Mi, 119–120
    Chinese Flank Steak &
        Onions, aka Mongolian
        Beef, 103
    Vietnamese Beef Stew, 44–45

Vietnamese
    Meatloaf, 111–112
Beer
    Korean Pork Wraps, 109–110
Belacan, 154
    Belacan Not-Fried
        Chicken, 88
    Eggplant Sambal, 78
Bell peppers
    Burmese Chili Chicken, 97
    Chicken Lo Mein, 18
    Drunken Noodles, 17
    Filipino Chicken Curry, 56
    Red Chicken Curry, 51
Black glutinous rice
    Black Sticky Rice Pudding, 126
Black sesame seeds
    Black Sesame
        Cheesecake, 129–130
    Tomato Salad, 145
Bok choy, 154
    Beef Nilaga, 36
    Bok Choy with
        Mushrooms, 149
    Chicken Lo Mein, 18
    Filipino Oxtail Peanut
        Stew, 37–38
Buna-Shimeji mushrooms, 154
    Tom Kha Gai, 26

C

Cabbage
    Chicken Devil Curry, 59–60
    Fresh Kimchi, 142–143
    Sticky Rice in Lotus
        Leaf, 13–14
Caramelization, 81
Cardamom pods, 154
    Beef Pho Noodle Soup, 30–31
    Beef Rendang, 61–62
    Braised Lamb
        Shanks, 113–114

Chicken Kurma, 64–65
Lamb Rogan Josh, 48
Lentil Soup, 34
Red Lentil Curry, 55
Spiced Potatoes, 74
Carrots
    Beef Kare Raisu from
        Scratch, 52–53
    Beef Nilaga, 36
    Braised Short Ribs, 102
    Brisket Banh Mi, 119–120
    Carrot Sambol, 144
    Chicken Kare Raisu, 54
    Green Papaya Salad, 146
    Mushroom Jook, 11
    Vietnamese Beef Stew, 44–45
Cashews
    Coconut Custard, 133–134
Cauliflower
    Spiced Cauliflower &
        Potatoes, 70
Chestnuts
    Korean Ginseng Chicken
        Soup, 27–28
Chicken, 81
    Belacan Not-Fried Chicken, 88
    Burmese Chili Chicken, 97
    Chicken Adobo, 82
    Chicken Arroz Caldo, 12
    Chicken Congee, 10
    Chicken Devil Curry, 59–60
    Chicken Kare Raisu, 54
    Chicken Kurma, 64–65
    Chicken Lo Mein, 18
    Chicken Teriyaki, 98
    Chicken Tikka Masala, 49–50
    Chinese Five-Spice Whole
        Chicken, 84–85
    Drunken Noodles, 17
    Filipino Chicken Curry, 56
    Ginger Chicken, 89
    Hainanese Chicken
        Rice, 90–91

Chicken (*Continued*)
Kerala Thattukada Chicken, 96
Khmer Curry, 63
Laksa Noodle Soup, 43
Laotian Chicken with
Mushrooms, 99
Malaysian Chicken Wings, 83
Red Chicken Curry, 51
Roast Chicken, 92
Shan Noodles, 19
Spicy Lemongrass Chicken, 93
Steamed Chicken in Coconut
Water, 94–95
Three-Cup Chicken, 86–87
Tom Kha Gai, 26
Chickpeas
Spicy Chickpeas &
Potatoes, 77
Chiles, dried red, 157
Beef Rendang, 61–62
Chicken Devil Curry, 59–60
Eggplant Sambal, 78
Pork Belly Curry, 57–58
Three-Cup Chicken, 86–87
Chiles, green
Carrot Sambol, 144
Red Lentil Curry, 55
Spiced Cauliflower &
Potatoes, 70
Chiles, red
Eggplant Sambal, 78
Ginger Chicken, 89
Green Papaya Salad, 146
Laksa Noodle Soup, 43
Steamed Chicken in Coconut
Water, 94–95
Vietnamese
Meatloaf, 111–112
Chinese black vinegar, 155
Chinese five-spice powder, 155
Chinese long beans
Filipino Oxtail Peanut
Stew, 37–38
Cilantro
Beef Pho Noodle Soup, 30–31
Braised Lamb
Shanks, 113–114
Brisket Banh Mi, 119–120

Cambodian Caramelized
Pork, 105
Chicken Congee, 10
Chicken Kurma, 64–65
Chicken Tikka Masala, 49–50
Eggplant & Thai Basil, 71
Ginger Chicken, 89
Green Papaya Salad, 146
Hainanese Chicken
Rice, 90–91
Laksa Noodle Soup, 43
Laotian Chicken with
Mushrooms, 99
Lentil Soup, 34
Pork Belly Curry, 57–58
Red Chicken Curry, 51
Roast Chicken, 92
Spiced Cauliflower &
Potatoes, 70
Spicy Lemongrass
Chicken, 93
Steamed Chicken in Coconut
Water, 94–95
Taiwanese Braised Pork Belly
Buns, 106–107
Thai Cucumber Relish, 141
Tomato Salad, 145
Tom Kha Gai, 26
Vietnamese Beef Stew, 44–45
Coconut
Beef Rendang, 61–62
Black Sticky Rice Pudding, 126
Carrot Sambol, 144
Indonesian Steamed Coconut
Cupcake, 131–132
Coconut milk, 155
Beef Rendang, 61–62
Black Sticky Rice Pudding, 126
Chicken Kurma, 64–65
Coconut Custard, 133–134
Filipino Chicken Curry, 56
Indonesian Braised Tofu, 79
Indonesian Steamed
Coconut
Cupcake, 131–132
Khmer Curry, 63
Laksa Noodle Soup, 43

Matcha & Coconut Mochi
Cake, 124–125
Red Chicken Curry, 51
Red Lentil Curry, 55
Tom Kha Gai, 26
Coconut water, 155
Ginger Chicken, 89
Steamed Chicken in Coconut
Water, 94–95
Vietnamese Beef Stew, 44–45
Coffee
Korean Pork Wraps, 109–110
Coriander powder, 155
Corn
Beef Kare Raisu from
Scratch, 52–53
Chicken Kare Raisu, 54
Drunken Noodles, 17
Shoyu Pork Ramen, 41–42
Cornish hens
Korean Ginseng Chicken
Soup, 27–28
Cream
Pumpkin Soup, 29
Cream cheese
Black Sesame
Cheesecake, 129–130
Cucumbers, English
Black Bean Sauce Noodles, 15
Brisket Banh Mi, 119–120
Hainanese Chicken
Rice, 90–91
Thai Cucumber Relish, 141
Vietnamese
Meatloaf, 111–112
Cumin, 155
Curries, 47
Beef Kare Raisu from
Scratch, 52–53
Beef Rendang, 61–62
Chicken Devil Curry, 59–60
Chicken Kare Raisu, 54
Chicken Kurma, 64–65
Chicken Tikka Masala, 49–50
Filipino Chicken Curry, 56
Khmer Curry, 63
Lamb Rogan Josh, 48

Curries (*Continued*)
    Pork Belly Curry, 57–58
    Red Chicken Curry, 51
    Red Lentil Curry, 55
Curry leaves, 156
    Kerala Thattukada Chicken, 96
    Red Lentil Curry, 55
    Spiced Potatoes, 74
    Spicy Chickpeas &
        Potatoes, 77
Curry powder, 156
Curry sauce mix, 156

D

Dangmyeon, 156
    Beef Short Rib Soup, 24–25
    Korean Oxtail Soup, 22–23
Dashi stock, 156
    Braised Pork Belly, 117–118
    Shoyu Pork Ramen, 41–42
    Simmered Pumpkin, 72
    Steamed Egg with Mushroom
        & Asparagus, 75–76
Desserts
    Asian Pear Upside-Down
        Cake, 135–136
    Black Sesame
        Cheesecake, 129–130
    Black Sticky Rice Pudding, 126
    Coconut Custard, 133–134
    Indonesian Steamed Coconut
        Cupcake, 131–132
    Mango Compote, 137
    Matcha & Coconut Mochi
        Cake, 124–125
    Sweet Rice Punch, 127–128
Doenjang, 157
    Korean Pork Wraps, 109–110
    Soybean Paste Stew, 32–33
Doubanjiang, 157
    Mapo Tofu, 68–69
Douchi (fermented black
    beans), 157
    Mapo Tofu, 68–69
Dressings
    Miso Salad Dressing, 150

E

Eggplant
    Eggplant & Thai Basil, 71
    Eggplant Sambal, 78
    Red Chicken Curry, 51
Eggs
    Asian Pear Upside-Down
        Cake, 135–136
    Black Sesame
        Cheesecake, 129–130
    Braised Pork Belly, 117–118
    Cambodian Caramelized
        Pork, 105
    Chicken Arroz Caldo, 12
    Coconut Custard, 133–134
    Indonesian Steamed Coconut
        Cupcake, 131–132
    Matcha & Coconut Mochi
        Cake, 124–125
    Shoyu Pork Ramen, 41–42
    Steamed Egg with Mushroom
        & Asparagus, 75–76
    Vietnamese
        Meatloaf, 111–112
8+ hours
    Beef Pho Noodle Soup, 30–31
    Beef Short Rib Soup, 24–25
    Black Sticky Rice Pudding, 126
    Braised Short Ribs, 102
    Brisket Banh Mi, 119–120
    Filipino Oxtail Peanut
        Stew, 37–38
    Korean Ginseng Chicken
        Soup, 27–28
    Korean Oxtail Soup, 22–23
    Spicy Chickpeas &
        Potatoes, 77
    Sticky Rice in Lotus
        Leaf, 13–14

F

Fennel, 157
Fish sauce, 157
    Beef Nilaga, 36
    Beef Pho Noodle Soup, 30–31

Belacan Not-Fried Chicken, 88
Brisket Banh Mi, 119–120
Burmese Chili Chicken, 97
Cambodian Caramelized
    Pork, 105
Chicken Arroz Caldo, 12
Drunken Noodles, 17
Eggplant & Thai Basil, 71
Filipino Chicken Curry, 56
Fresh Kimchi, 142–143
Ginger Chicken, 89
Green Papaya Salad, 146
Khmer Curry, 63
Kimchi Stew, 39–40
Korean Oxtail Soup, 22–23
Laksa Noodle Soup, 43
Laotian Chicken with
    Mushrooms, 99
Malaysian Chicken Wings, 83
Pork Belly Curry, 57–58
Red Chicken Curry, 51
Roast Chicken, 92
Shan Noodles, 19
Spicy Lemongrass
    Chicken, 93
Spicy Radish Salad, 148
Steamed Chicken in Coconut
    Water, 94–95
Tom Kha Gai, 26
Vietnamese
    Meatloaf, 111–112

G

Galangal, 157
    Beef Rendang, 61–62
    Chicken Devil Curry, 59–60
    Indonesian Braised Tofu, 79
    Khmer Curry, 63
    Pork Belly Curry, 57–58
    Steamed Chicken in Coconut
        Water, 94–95
    Tom Kha Gai, 26
Garam masala, 158
Ginger, 158
    Beef Pho Noodle Soup, 30–31
    Beef Rendang, 61–62

Ginger (*Continued*)
  Braised Lamb
    Shanks, 113–114
  Braised Pork Belly, 117–118
  Braised Pork Shoulder, 104
  Braised Short Ribs, 102
  Burmese Chili Chicken, 97
  Chicken Arroz Caldo, 12
  Chicken Congee, 10
  Chicken Kurma, 64–65
  Chicken Tikka Masala, 49–50
  Chinese Five-Spice Whole
    Chicken, 84–85
  Chinese Flank Steak &
    Onions, aka Mongolian
    Beef, 103
  Drunken Noodles, 17
  Fresh Kimchi, 142–143
  Ginger Chicken, 89
  Hainanese Chicken
    Rice, 90–91
  Kerala Thattukada Chicken, 96
  Korean Pork Wraps, 109–110
  Lamb Rogan Josh, 48
  Laotian Chicken with
    Mushrooms, 99
  Lentil Soup, 34
  Malaysian Chicken Wings, 83
  Mapo Tofu, 68–69
  Miso Salad Dressing, 150
  Pork Belly Curry, 57–58
  Pumpkin Soup, 29
  Shan Noodles, 19
  Shoyu Pork Ramen, 41–42
  Spiced Cauliflower &
    Potatoes, 70
  Spicy Baby Back Pork
    Ribs, 121
  Spicy Chickpeas &
    Potatoes, 77
  Sticky Rice in Lotus
    Leaf, 13–14
  Sweet-and-Sour
    Ribs, 115–116
  Taiwanese Braised Pork Belly
    Buns, 106–107
  Three-Cup Chicken, 86–87
Ginseng, 158

Gluten-free
  Beef Nilaga, 36
  Beef Rendang, 61–62
  Belacan Not-Fried Chicken, 88
  Black Sticky Rice Pudding, 126
  Braised Lamb
    Shanks, 113–114
  Burmese Chili Chicken, 97
  Carrot Sambol, 144
  Chicken Arroz Caldo, 12
  Chicken Devil Curry, 59–60
  Chicken Kare Raisu, 54
  Chicken Kurma, 64–65
  Chicken Tikka Masala, 49–50
  Coconut Custard, 133–134
  Eggplant Sambal, 78
  Filipino Chicken Curry, 56
  Filipino Oxtail Peanut
    Stew, 37–38
  Fresh Kimchi, 142–143
  Green Papaya Salad, 146
  Kerala Thattukada
    Chicken, 96
  Khmer Curry, 63
  Kimchi Stew, 39–40
  Korean Ginseng Chicken
    Soup, 27–28
  Korean Oxtail Soup, 22–23
  Laksa Noodle Soup, 43
  Lamb Rogan Josh, 48
  Laotian Chicken with
    Mushrooms, 99
  Lentil Soup, 34
  Mango Compote, 137
  Matcha & Coconut Mochi
    Cake, 124–125
  Pumpkin Soup, 29
  Red Chicken Curry, 51
  Red Lentil Curry, 55
  Roast Chicken, 92
  Soybean Paste Stew, 32–33
  Spiced Cauliflower &
    Potatoes, 70
  Spiced Potatoes, 74
  Spicy Chickpeas &
    Potatoes, 77
  Spicy Lemongrass Chicken, 93
  Spicy Radish Salad, 148

  Steamed Chicken in Coconut
    Water, 94–95
  Thai Cucumber Relish, 141
  Tomato Salad, 145
  Tom Kha Gai, 26
  Vietnamese Beef Stew, 44–45
  Vietnamese
    Meatloaf, 111–112
  Yellow Mung Beans & Rice, 16
Gochugaru, 158
  Beef Short Rib Soup, 24–25
  Fresh Kimchi, 142–143
  Korean Oxtail Soup, 22–23
  Soybean Paste Stew, 32–33
  Soy Silken Tofu, 73
  Spicy Radish Salad, 148
Gochujang, 158
  Kimchi Stew, 39–40
  Korean Pork Wraps, 109–110
  Spicy Baby Back Pork
    Ribs, 121
Greek yogurt
  Chicken Tikka Masala, 49–50
Green beans
  Filipino Oxtail Peanut
    Stew, 37–38
  Red Chicken Curry, 51
Green papaya, 159
  Green Papaya Salad, 146

H

Hobak (Korean gray squash)
  Soybean Paste Stew, 32–33
Hoisin sauce, 159
  Beef Pho Noodle Soup, 30–31
  Chinese-Style "Roasted"
    Lamb, 108

J

Jaggery, 159
  Coconut Custard, 133–134
Jalapeños
  Beef Pho Noodle Soup, 30–31
  Brisket Banh Mi, 119–120

Jalapeños (*Continued*)
　Chicken Devil Curry, 59–60
　Soybean Paste Stew, 32–33
Jasmine rice
　Hainanese Chicken
　　Rice, 90–91
Jjajang, 159
　Black Bean Sauce
　　Noodles, 15
Jjajangmyeon noodles
　Black Bean Sauce Noodles, 15
Jujubes (Chinese red dates), 159
　Korean Ginseng Chicken
　　Soup, 27–28
　Sweet Rice Punch, 127–128

K

Kabocha squash
　Simmered Pumpkin, 72
Kaffir lime leaves, 159
　Beef Rendang, 61–62
　Khmer Curry, 63
　Red Chicken Curry, 51
　Steamed Chicken in Coconut
　　Water, 94–95
　Tom Kha Gai, 26
Karashi, 159
Kashmiri chili powder, 160
Kecap manis, 160
　Braised Pork Shoulder, 104
　Hainanese Chicken
　　Rice, 90–91
　Indonesian Braised Tofu, 79
Kimchi, 160
　Fresh Kimchi, 142–143
　Kimchi Stew, 39–40
Konbu (kelp)
　Soybean Paste Stew, 32–33

L

Laksa paste, 160
　Laksa Noodle Soup, 43
Lamb
　Braised Lamb
　　Shanks, 113–114

Chinese-Style "Roasted"
　　Lamb, 108
　Lamb Rogan Josh, 48
Lemongrass, 160
　Beef Rendang, 61–62
　Brisket Banh Mi, 119–120
　Khmer Curry, 63
　Pork Belly Curry, 57–58
　Spicy Lemongrass Chicken, 93
　Steamed Chicken in Coconut
　　Water, 94–95
　Tom Kha Gai, 26
　Vietnamese Beef Stew, 44–45
Lemons and lemon juice
　Beef Nilaga, 36
　Braised Pork Shoulder, 104
　Chicken Arroz Caldo, 12
　Chicken Tikka Masala, 49–50
　Kerala Thattukada Chicken, 96
　Lentil Soup, 34
　Mango Compote, 137
　Roast Chicken, 92
　Spicy Chickpeas &
　　Potatoes, 77
Lentils, red
　Red Lentil Curry, 55
Lentils, yellow
　Lentil Soup, 34
Lettuce
　Korean Pork Wraps, 109–110
Limes and lime juice
　Beef Pho Noodle Soup, 30–31
　Belacan Not-Fried Chicken, 88
　Brisket Banh Mi, 119–120
　Carrot Sambol, 144
　Chicken Kurma, 64–65
　Green Papaya Salad, 146
　Hainanese Chicken
　　Rice, 90–91
　Laksa Noodle Soup, 43
　Mango Compote, 137
　Miso Salad Dressing, 150
　Roast Chicken, 92
　Spiced Potatoes, 74
　Steamed Chicken in Coconut
　　Water, 94–95
　Tomato Salad, 145
　Tom Kha Gai, 26

Vietnamese
　　Meatloaf, 111–112
Lo mein noodles
　Chicken Lo Mein, 18
Long-grain rice
　Chicken Congee, 10
　Hainanese Chicken
　　Rice, 90–91
Lotus leaves, dried, 157
　Sticky Rice in Lotus
　　Leaf, 13–14
Lotus root
　Stir-Fried Lotus Root, 147

M

Mangoes
　Mango Compote, 137
Matcha powder, 161
　Matcha & Coconut Mochi
　　Cake, 124–125
Mint
　Beef Pho Noodle Soup, 30–31
　Green Papaya Salad, 146
Mirin, 161
　Braised Pork Belly, 117–118
　Braised Short Ribs, 102
　Chicken Teriyaki, 98
　Shoyu Pork Ramen, 41–42
　Spicy Baby Back Pork
　　Ribs, 121
　Stir-Fried Lotus Root, 147
Miso, 161
　Miso Salad Dressing, 150
Mochiko (glutinous sweet rice
　　flour), 161
　Fresh Kimchi, 142–143
　Matcha & Coconut Mochi
　　Cake, 124–125
Moong dal (split yellow
　　mung beans)
　Yellow Mung Beans & Rice, 16
Mu (Korean radish), 161
Mung bean sprouts
　Beef Pho Noodle Soup, 30–31
　Shoyu Pork Ramen, 41–42

Mung bean threads, 161
  Vietnamese
    Meatloaf, 111–112
Mushrooms. *See* Buna-Shimeji
    mushrooms; Shiitake
    mushrooms; Wood ear
    mushrooms
Mustard greens, pickled, 162
  Shan Noodles, 19
  Taiwanese Braised Pork Belly
    Buns, 106–107
Myeolchi, 161
  Soybean Paste Stew, 32–33

N

Noodles, 9. *See also* Dangmyeon;
    Jjajangmyeon noodles;
    Lo mein noodles; Mung
    bean threads; Ramen
    noodles; Rice noodles;
    Udon noodles
Nori
  Mushroom Jook, 11
  Shoyu Pork Ramen, 41–42
Nut-free
  Asian Pear Upside-Down
    Cake, 135–136
  Beef Kare Raisu from
    Scratch, 52–53
  Beef Nilaga, 36
  Beef Pho Noodle Soup, 30–31
  Beef Rendang, 61–62
  Beef Short Rib Soup, 24–25
  Belacan Not-Fried Chicken, 88
  Black Bean Sauce Noodles, 15
  Black Sesame
    Cheesecake, 129–130
  Black Sticky Rice Pudding, 126
  Bok Choy with
    Mushrooms, 149
  Braised Lamb
    Shanks, 113–114
  Braised Pork Belly, 117–118
  Braised Pork Shoulder, 104
  Brisket Banh Mi, 119–120
  Burmese Chili Chicken, 97

Cambodian Caramelized
    Pork, 105
Carrot Sambol, 144
Chicken Adobo, 82
Chicken Arroz Caldo, 12
Chicken Kare Raisu, 54
Chicken Lo Mein, 18
Chicken Teriyaki, 98
Chicken Tikka Masala, 49–50
Chinese Five-Spice whole
    Chicken, 84–85
Chinese Flank Steak & Onions,
    aka Mongolian Beef, 103
Chinese-Style "Roasted"
    Lamb, 108
Drunken Noodles, 17
Eggplant & Thai Basil, 71
Eggplant Sambal, 78
Filipino Chicken Curry, 56
Fresh Kimchi, 142–143
Ginger Chicken, 89
Hainanese Chicken
    Rice, 90–91
Hot-and-Sour Soup, 35
Indonesian Braised Tofu, 79
Indonesian Steamed
    Coconut
    Cupcake, 131–132
Kerala Thattukada Chicken, 96
Khmer Curry, 63
Kimchi Stew, 39–40
Korean Ginseng Chicken
    Soup, 27–28
Korean Oxtail Soup, 22–23
Korean Pork Wraps, 109–110
Laksa Noodle Soup, 43
Lamb Rogan Josh, 48
Laotian Chicken with
    Mushrooms, 99
Lentil Soup, 34
Malaysian Chicken Wings, 83
Mango Compote, 137
Matcha & Coconut Mochi
    Cake, 124–125
Mushroom Jook, 11
Pork Belly Curry, 57–58
Pumpkin Soup, 29

Red Chicken Curry, 51
Red Lentil Curry, 55
Roast Chicken, 92
Shoyu Pork Ramen, 41–42
Simmered Pumpkin, 72
Soybean Paste Stew, 32–33
Soy Silken Tofu, 73
Spiced Cauliflower &
    Potatoes, 70
Spiced Potatoes, 74
Spicy Baby Back Pork
    Ribs, 121
Spicy Chickpeas &
    Potatoes, 77
Spicy Lemongrass Chicken, 93
Spicy Radish Salad, 148
Steamed Egg with Mushroom
    & Asparagus, 75–76
Sticky Rice in Lotus
    Leaf, 13–14
Stir-Fried Asparagus, 140
Stir-Fried Lotus Root, 147
Sweet-and-Sour
    Ribs, 115–116
Thai Cucumber Relish, 141
Three-Cup Chicken, 86–87
Tom Kha Gai, 26
Vietnamese Beef Stew, 44–45
Vietnamese
    Meatloaf, 111–112
Yellow Mung Beans & Rice, 16

O

Oligodang, 162
  Fresh Kimchi, 142–143
Oxtails
  Filipino Oxtail Peanut
    Stew, 37–38
  Korean Oxtail Soup, 22–23
Oyster sauce, 162
  Bok Choy with
    Mushrooms, 149
  Chicken Lo Mein, 18
  Chinese Flank Steak & Onions,
    aka Mongolian Beef, 103
  Drunken Noodles, 17

Oyster sauce (*Continued*)
    Eggplant & Thai Basil, 71
    Sticky Rice in Lotus
      Leaf, 13–14
    Stir-Fried Asparagus, 140

P

Palm sugar, 162
    Beef Rendang, 61–62
    Black Sticky Rice Pudding, 126
    Cambodian Caramelized
      Pork, 105
    Coconut Custard, 133–134
    Khmer Curry, 63
    Pork Belly Curry, 57–58
    Red Chicken Curry, 51
Pan searing, 2–3
Patis, 162
Peanut butter
    Filipino Oxtail Peanut
      Stew, 37–38
Peanuts
    Chicken Congee, 10
    Green Papaya Salad, 146
    Shan Noodles, 19
    Steamed Chicken in Coconut
      Water, 94–95
    Taiwanese Braised Pork Belly
      Buns, 106–107
    Tomato Salad, 145
Peas
    Beef Kare Raisu from
      Scratch, 52–53
    Chicken Kare Raisu, 54
Pechay, 162
    Beef Nilaga, 36
    Filipino Oxtail Peanut
      Stew, 37–38
Poblano chiles
    Burmese Chili Chicken, 97
Pork. *See also* Sausage
    Black Bean Sauce Noodles, 15
    Braised Pork Belly, 117–118
    Braised Pork Shoulder, 104
    Cambodian Caramelized
      Pork, 105

    Khmer Curry, 63
    Kimchi Stew, 39–40
    Korean Pork Wraps, 109–110
    Pork Belly Curry, 57–58
    Shoyu Pork Ramen, 41–42
    Spicy Baby Back Pork
      Ribs, 121
    Sweet-and-Sour
      Ribs, 115–116
    Taiwanese Braised Pork
      Belly Buns, 106–107
    Vietnamese
      Meatloaf, 111–112
Potatoes. *See also* Sweet
    potatoes
    Beef Kare Raisu from
      Scratch, 52–53
    Beef Nilaga, 36
    Black Bean Sauce
      Noodles, 15
    Braised Short Ribs, 102
    Chicken Devil Curry, 59–60
    Chicken Kare Raisu, 54
    Chicken Kurma, 64–65
    Spiced Cauliflower &
      Potatoes, 70
    Spiced Potatoes, 74
    Spicy Chickpeas &
      Potatoes, 77
Prahok, 162
    Khmer Curry, 63
Pumpkin
    Khmer Curry, 63
    Pumpkin Soup, 29

Q

Quick prep
    Belacan Not-Fried Chicken, 88
    Black Bean Sauce Noodles, 15
    Black Sticky Rice Pudding, 126
    Bok Choy with
      Mushrooms, 149
    Burmese Chili Chicken, 97
    Carrot Sambol, 144
    Chicken Adobo, 82
    Chicken Arroz Caldo, 12

    Chicken Congee, 10
    Chicken Kare Raisu, 54
    Chicken Lo Mein, 18
    Chicken Teriyaki, 98
    Chicken Tikka Masala, 49–50
    Chinese Five-Spice whole
      Chicken, 84–85
    Coconut Custard, 133–134
    Drunken Noodles, 17
    Eggplant & Thai Basil, 71
    Filipino Chicken Curry, 56
    Ginger Chicken, 89
    Green Papaya Salad, 146
    Hainanese Chicken
      Rice, 90–91
    Hot-and-Sour Soup, 35
    Indonesian Braised Tofu, 79
    Indonesian Steamed Coconut
      Cupcake, 131–132
    Kerala Thattukada Chicken, 96
    Laksa Noodle Soup, 43
    Lamb Rogan Josh, 48
    Lentil Soup, 34
    Malaysian Chicken Wings, 83
    Mango Compote, 137
    Mapo Tofu, 68–69
    Miso Salad Dressing, 150
    Pork Belly Curry, 57–58
    Pumpkin Soup, 29
    Red Chicken Curry, 51
    Red Lentil Curry, 55
    Roast Chicken, 92
    Shan Noodles, 19
    Simmered Pumpkin, 72
    Soy Silken Tofu, 73
    Spiced Cauliflower &
      Potatoes, 70
    Spiced Potatoes, 74
    Spicy Baby Back Pork
      Ribs, 121
    Spicy Lemongrass Chicken, 93
    Spicy Radish Salad, 148
    Steamed Chicken in Coconut
      Water, 94–95
    Steamed Egg with Mushroom
      & Asparagus, 75–76
    Stir-Fried Asparagus, 140

Quick prep (*Continued*)
    Stir-Fried Lotus Root, 147
    Sweet Rice Punch, 127–128
    Taiwanese Braised Pork Belly
       Buns, 106–107
    Thai Cucumber Relish, 141
    Three-Cup Chicken, 86–87
    Tom Kha Gai, 26
    Vietnamese Beef Stew, 44–45
    Yellow Mung Beans & Rice, 16

R

Radishes
    Beef Short Rib Soup, 24–25
    Braised Short Ribs, 102
    Spicy Radish Salad, 148
Ramen noodles
    Shoyu Pork Ramen, 41–42
Red curry paste, 163
    Red Chicken Curry, 51
Rice, 9. *See also* Basmati rice;
    Black glutinous rice;
    Jasmine rice; Long-grain
    rice; Sticky rice (sweet rice)
Rice noodles, 163
    Beef Pho Noodle Soup, 30–31
    Drunken Noodles, 17
    Laksa Noodle Soup, 43
    Shan Noodles, 19
Rice vinegar, seasoned, 163

S

Saba bananas, 163
    Beef Nilaga, 36
Sake, 163
    Braised Pork Belly, 117–118
    Chicken Teriyaki, 98
    Shoyu Pork Ramen, 41–42
    Simmered Pumpkin, 72
    Stir-Fried Lotus Root, 147
Salads
    Green Papaya Salad, 146
    Spicy Radish Salad, 148
    Tomato Salad, 145
Sambal oelek, 163
    Braised Pork Shoulder, 104

Sausage
    Chicken Devil Curry, 59–60
    Sticky Rice in Lotus
       Leaf, 13–14
Sautéing, 2–3
Scallions
    Beef Short Rib Soup, 24–25
    Braised Pork Belly, 117–118
    Chicken Arroz Caldo, 12
    Chicken Congee, 10
    Chicken Lo Mein, 18
    Chicken Teriyaki, 98
    Chinese Five-Spice whole
       Chicken, 84–85
    Chinese Flank Steak & Onions,
       aka Mongolian Beef, 103
    Drunken Noodles, 17
    Fresh Kimchi, 142–143
    Ginger Chicken, 89
    Hainanese Chicken
       Rice, 90–91
    Hot-and-Sour Soup, 35
    Kimchi Stew, 39–40
    Korean Ginseng Chicken
       Soup, 27–28
    Korean Oxtail Soup, 22–23
    Korean Pork Wraps, 109–110
    Mapo Tofu, 68–69
    Mushroom Jook, 11
    Shan Noodles, 19
    Shoyu Pork Ramen, 41–42
    Soybean Paste Stew, 32–33
    Soy Silken Tofu, 73
    Spicy Lemongrass Chicken, 93
    Spicy Radish Salad, 148
    Steamed Chicken in Coconut
       Water, 94–95
    Steamed Egg with Mushroom
       & Asparagus, 75–76
    Three-Cup Chicken, 86–87
    Vietnamese
       Meatloaf, 111–112
Sesame oil, 163
Sesame seeds. *See also* Black
    sesame seeds
    Black Sticky Rice Pudding, 126
    Chicken Teriyaki, 98

Fresh Kimchi, 142–143
Korean Pork Wraps, 109–110
Mushroom Jook, 11
Soy Silken Tofu, 73
Spicy Radish Salad, 148
Stir-Fried Asparagus, 140
Stir-Fried Lotus Root, 147
Shallots
    Braised Pork Shoulder, 104
    Brisket Banh Mi, 119–120
    Cambodian Caramelized
       Pork, 105
    Chicken Congee, 10
    Chicken Kurma, 64–65
    Chicken Lo Mein, 18
    Drunken Noodles, 17
    Eggplant Sambal, 78
    Green Papaya Salad, 146
    Hainanese Chicken
       Rice, 90–91
    Indonesian Braised Tofu, 79
    Kerala Thattukada Chicken, 96
    Khmer Curry, 63
    Pork Belly Curry, 57–58
    Spicy Lemongrass Chicken, 93
    Sticky Rice in Lotus
       Leaf, 13–14
    Thai Cucumber Relish, 141
    Tom Kha Gai, 26
    Vietnamese
       Meatloaf, 111–112
Shaoxing wine, 163
    Chinese Flank Steak &
       Onions, aka Mongolian
       Beef, 103
    Chinese-Style "Roasted"
       Lamb, 108
    Sticky Rice in Lotus
       Leaf, 13–14
    Sweet-and-Sour
       Ribs, 115–116
    Taiwanese Braised Pork Belly
       Buns, 106–107
    Three-Cup Chicken, 86–87
Shichimi, 164
    Shoyu Pork Ramen, 41–42
    sichuan peppercorns, 164

Shiitake mushrooms
  Bok Choy with
    Mushrooms, 149
  Hot-and-Sour Soup, 35
  Laotian Chicken with
    Mushrooms, 99
  Mapo Tofu, 68–69
  Mushroom Jook, 11
  Soybean Paste Stew, 32–33
  Steamed Egg with Mushroom
    & Asparagus, 75–76
  Sticky Rice in Lotus
    Leaf, 13–14
Short-grain rice
  Chicken Arroz Caldo, 12
  Mushroom Jook, 11
  Sweet Rice Punch, 127–128
Shrimp
  Laksa Noodle Soup, 43
  Soybean Paste Stew, 32–33
Shrimp paste. See also Belacan
  Khmer Curry, 63
  Pork Belly Curry, 57–58
Side dishes. See also Salads
  Bok Choy with
    Mushrooms, 149
  Carrot Sambol, 144
  Fresh Kimchi, 142–143
  Stir-Fried Asparagus, 140
  Stir-Fried Lotus Root, 147
  Thai Cucumber Relish, 141
Slow cookers and cooking
  about, 6
  benefits of for Asian
    cuisine, 2–3
  dos and don'ts, 7
Soups. See also Stews
  Beef Pho Noodle Soup, 30–31
  Beef Short Rib Soup, 24–25
  Hot-and-Sour Soup, 35
  Korean Ginseng Chicken
    Soup, 27–28
  Korean Oxtail Soup, 22–23
  Laksa Noodle Soup, 43
  Lentil Soup, 34
  Pumpkin Soup, 29
  Shoyu Pork Ramen, 41–42

Tom Kha Gai, 26
Sour cream
  Black Sesame
    Cheesecake, 129–130
Soy-free
  Asian Pear Upside-Down
    Cake, 135–136
  Beef Nilaga, 36
  Beef Rendang, 61–62
  Belacan Not-Fried
    Chicken, 88
  Black Sesame
    Cheesecake, 129–130
  Black Sticky Rice Pudding, 126
  Braised Lamb
    Shanks, 113–114
  Burmese Chili Chicken, 97
  Carrot Sambol, 144
  Chicken Arroz Caldo, 12
  Chicken Congee, 10
  Chicken Kare Raisu, 54
  Chicken Kurma, 64–65
  Coconut Custard, 133–134
  Eggplant Sambal, 78
  Filipino Chicken Curry, 56
  Filipino Oxtail Peanut
    Stew, 37–38
  Fresh Kimchi, 142–143
  Green Papaya Salad, 146
  Indonesian Steamed Coconut
    Cupcake, 131–132
  Kerala Thattukada
    Chicken, 96
  Khmer Curry, 63
  Korean Ginseng Chicken
    Soup, 27–28
  Korean Oxtail Soup, 22–23
  Laksa Noodle Soup, 43
  Lamb Rogan Josh, 48
  Laotian Chicken with
    Mushrooms, 99
  Lentil Soup, 34
  Mango Compote, 137
  Matcha & Coconut Mochi
    Cake, 124–125
  Pumpkin Soup, 29
  Red Chicken Curry, 51

Red Lentil Curry, 55
  Roast Chicken, 92
  Spiced Cauliflower &
    Potatoes, 70
  Spiced Potatoes, 74
  Spicy Chickpeas &
    Potatoes, 77
  Spicy Lemongrass
    Chicken, 93
  Spicy Radish Salad, 148
  Steamed Chicken in
    Coconut Water, 94–95
  Sweet Rice Punch, 127–128
  Thai Cucumber Relish, 141
  Tomato Salad, 145
  Tom Kha Gai, 26
  Vietnamese Beef Stew, 44–45
  Vietnamese
    Meatloaf, 111–112
  Yellow Mung Beans & Rice, 16
Soy sauce, 164
  Beef Short Rib Soup, 24–25
  Braised Pork Belly, 117–118
  Braised Short Ribs, 102
  Brisket Banh Mi, 119–120
  Cambodian Caramelized
    Pork, 105
  Chicken Adobo, 82
  Chicken Congee, 10
  Chicken Lo Mein, 18
  Chicken Teriyaki, 98
  Chinese Five-Spice whole
    Chicken, 84–85
  Chinese Flank Steak &
    Onions, aka Mongolian
    Beef, 103
  Chinese-Style "Roasted"
    Lamb, 108
  Drunken Noodles, 17
  Eggplant & Thai Basil, 71
  Hot-and-Sour Soup, 35
  Malaysian Chicken Wings, 83
  Mushroom Jook, 11
  Shan Noodles, 19
  Shoyu Pork Ramen, 41–42
  Simmered Pumpkin, 72
  Soy Silken Tofu, 73

Soy sauce (*Continued*)
    Spicy Baby Back Pork
        Ribs, 121
    Steamed Egg with
        Mushroom &
        Asparagus, 75–76
    Stir-Fried Lotus Root, 147
    Sweet-and-Sour
        Ribs, 115–116
    Yellow Mung Beans & Rice, 16
Soy sauce, dark, 156
    Braised Pork Shoulder, 104
    Ginger Chicken, 89
    Malaysian Chicken
        Wings, 83
    Pork Belly Curry, 57–58
    Sticky Rice in Lotus
        Leaf, 13–14
    Taiwanese Braised Pork
        Belly Buns, 106–107
Soy sauce, light, 160
    Hot-and-Sour Soup, 35
    Taiwanese Braised Pork Belly
        Buns, 106–107
    Three-Cup Chicken, 86–87
Squash. *See* Hobak (Korean
    gray squash); Kabocha
    squash; Pumpkin
Sriracha, 164
    Beef Pho Noodle Soup, 30–31
    Hainanese Chicken
        Rice, 90–91
Star anise, 164
    Beef Pho Noodle Soup, 30–31
    Beef Rendang, 61–62
    Brisket Banh Mi, 119–120
    Cambodian Caramelized
        Pork, 105
    Taiwanese Braised
        Pork Belly Buns, 106–107
    Vietnamese Beef Stew, 44–45
Steamed white buns, 164
    Taiwanese Braised Pork Belly
        Buns, 106–107
Stews. *See also* Curries
    Beef Nilaga, 36
    Filipino Oxtail Peanut
        Stew, 37–38

    Kimchi Stew, 39–40
    Vietnamese Beef Stew, 44–45
    Soybean Paste Stew, 32–33
Sticky rice (sweet rice), 164
    Korean Ginseng Chicken
        Soup, 27–28
    Sticky Rice in Lotus
        Leaf, 13–14
Sweet potatoes
    Filipino Chicken Curry, 56
Sweet rice. *See* Sticky rice
    (sweet rice)

T

Tamarind paste, 165
    Beef Rendang, 61–62
    Pork Belly Curry, 57–58
Tamarind water, 165
    Eggplant Sambal, 78
    Indonesian Braised Tofu, 79
Thai basil, 165
    Beef Pho Noodle
        Soup, 30–31
    Drunken Noodles, 17
    Eggplant & Thai Basil, 71
    Red Chicken Curry, 51
    Three-Cup Chicken, 86–87
Thai chiles/Thai bird's eye
    chiles, 165
    Drunken Noodles, 17
    Eggplant & Thai Basil, 71
    Spicy Lemongrass Chicken, 93
    Thai Cucumber Relish, 141
    Tom Kha Gai, 26
Thickening agents, 2–3
Tofu
    Hot-and-Sour Soup, 35
    Indonesian Braised Tofu, 79
    Kimchi Stew, 39–40
    Laksa Noodle Soup, 43
    Mapo Tofu, 68–69
    Soybean Paste Stew, 32–33
    Soy Silken Tofu, 73
Tomatoes
    Braised Lamb
        Shanks, 113–114

    Carrot Sambol, 144
    Chicken Devil Curry, 59–60
    Chicken Tikka
        Masala, 49–50
    Shan Noodles, 19
    Spiced Cauliflower &
        Potatoes, 70
    Spicy Chickpeas &
        Potatoes, 77
    Steamed Chicken in
        Coconut Water, 94–95
    Tomato Salad, 145
    Tom Kha Gai, 26
    Yellow Mung Beans & Rice, 16
Tonkatsu sauce, 165
    Beef Kare Raisu from
        Scratch, 52–53
Turmeric, 165

U

Udon noodles
    Black Bean Sauce
        Noodles, 15

V

Vegan
    Black Sticky Rice Pudding, 126
    Carrot Sambol, 144
    Indonesian Braised Tofu, 79
    Lentil Soup, 34
    Mango Compote, 137
    Mapo Tofu, 68–69
    Miso Salad Dressing, 150
    Soy Silken Tofu, 73
    Spiced Cauliflower &
        Potatoes, 70
    Spicy Chickpeas &
        Potatoes, 77
    Stir-Fried Lotus Root, 147
    Sweet Rice Punch, 127–128
    Thai Cucumber Relish, 141
    Tomato Salad, 145
    Yellow Mung Beans & Rice, 16
Vegetarian
    Spiced Potatoes, 74

W

Wood ear mushrooms, 165
    Hot-and-Sour Soup, 35
    Vietnamese
        Meatloaf, 111–112

Y

Yeotgireum-garu
    (malted barley flour)
    Sweet Rice Punch, 127–128
Yogurt. *See also* Greek yogurt
    Braised Lamb
        Shanks, 113–114
    Lamb Rogan Josh, 48

Z

Zucchini
    Black Bean Sauce Noodles, 15
    Mushroom Jook, 11

ACKNOWLEDGMENTS

There were many people who participated on this incredible journey, and I could not have done this without their support.

To my mom, dad, grandmother, and grandfather: Although not all of you are with me today (miss you 할머니 and 할아버지), you are not only my family but a representation of what courage is. Your entire lives were dedicated to supporting our family, working in difficult conditions in a foreign land to make a better future for your children and grandchildren. We kids knew times were hard growing up, but we were also able to "check out" by going to school, playing Nintendo, and taking piano and art lessons while you worked ruthless hours. Your courage is what I see most and will forever hold in my heart.

Dear Brad, what in the world did you get yourself into? You married a born-sarcastic skeptic (ahem . . . yes, that's me) and turned me around with your insanely huge heart. You are always there every step of the way, and have given me solid footing to stand on with your support, kindness, and honesty. Needless to say, there were a lot of dishes during this project and you dove right in to help. You made last-minute grocery store runs for me during some of my freak-out moments, and you did it all with no complaints. Sometimes I asked myself, "Where did this guy come from?!" Because even though I would do anything for you, I don't know if I could ever do it with such grace and style as you do. You are the positive force in my life. No wonder I fell head over heels for you.

When I was a kid, I begged for a sibling for years. Denise, I know that all my annoying begging and prayers were answered when you came along. Not just from the act of you being born, but because you are the coolest sister a sister could ask for. No other friendship compares to the relationship I have with you, and I am incredibly thankful for our sisterhood.

To my son, Ben: You are the sweetest thing in my life even though you were my toughest food critic. I am so lucky to be your mom and love your incredible mind, creativity, and humor. Thank you for your encouraging words and for helping me out in the kitchen, kiddo.

To the crew at Callisto Media: Thank you for believing in this book and for giving me this incredible opportunity. Meg, you knew I could do this project before I even knew. Having your support made me feel like this was all possible. Kim, I am so thankful for your guidance and leadership on this journey. I couldn't have asked for a better editor.

My amazing in-laws and friends: You are a community of kindness, talent, inspiration, and love. You are the best cheerleaders a gal can have. I am grateful to have you all in my life.

ABOUT THE AUTHOR

NANCY CHO followed her passion for art and food as an editor and recipe developer for *Anthology* magazine, where she sought flavors and ingredients inspired by memories of her childhood. Nancy is constantly searching for dishes that inspire others to enjoy the best of Asian cuisine. Nancy lives in the San Francisco Bay Area with her husband, son, and eccentric dog.

CPSIA information can be obtained
at www.ICGtesting.com
Printed in the USA
BVHW02s0842120618
518845BV00016B/122/P